NINJA TRUTHS AND MYTHS

VOLUME II

Newly Revised, Updated and Expanded!

By author Lex Lyon

www.lexlyonbooks.weebly.com[1]

PLEASE NOTE: The symbols on the front cover represent the actual word for "Ninja" in Japanese.

---

1. http://www.lexlyonbooks.weebly.com

CHAPTERS

NINJA PORTRAYAL

They are often portrayed in modern culture as cold-blooded assassins, garbed in black, who, armed with Samurai swords, throwing stars and nunchucks, appear out of nowhere in the shadows of night to sever the heads of their chosen victims without mercy.

These agents are even said to possess magical powers to include invisibility and walking on water, along with exhibiting such dazzling physical skills that they could easily rank world class in Olympic events such as gymnastics and track and field.

You even hear tongue-in-cheek statements in pictures such as "Only a Ninja can kill another Ninja!". That kind of hoopla might be fine for entertaining the younger audiences who love their super hero comic books, video games and Teenage Ninja Turtle flicks. But what about the adult crowd (like the author) who prefers a good dose of historical accuracy in their motion pictures, books, etc. After all, you have probably heard the saying that "truth is stranger than fiction."

The author became fascinated with them back in the decade of the 1980's when their craze in America had reached its peak. Ever since then I have set about consuming every book, article, and documentary I could feast my eyes upon.

What I discovered about them was actually quite surprising. Their reputation has been highly dramatized by misconception and the popular media. Sure, it may be more exciting to portray them as sword-slinging roof hopping executioners with mystical abilities.

But let's get real!

Now I'd like to share with you what I've learned. Here is the summation of all that research. And yes, I have found that truth truly is stranger than fiction.

FILM

The Famous Bond Film

The 1967 James Bond movie "You Only Live Twice" starring Sean Connery, which set into action the door to the initial exposure of ninjas to the American public, did not open in theaters without its share of controversy.

According to a quote from Black Belt Magazine, August 1967, the World's Leading Magazine of Self-defense:

"The results proved something less than successful, and touched off one of the many controversies that plagued the movies producers, Eon productions, throughout the two months of filming in Japan. There are only half a dozen or so authentic scholars and specialists in ninjutsu (the self-defense art of the ninja) still around in Japan today. And all of these experts washed their hands of the movie production on the ground that the film-makers failed to give a factual representation of the art of ninjitsu."

Other Films That Followed

Many would eventually jump on this band wagon such as actor/martial artists Chuck Norris in 'The Octagon' (1980), and Sho Kosugi in 'Revenge of the Ninja'.

While these productions may be highly entering, they too, for the sake of dramatization on the silver screen, played up many of the exaggerated stunts and gimmicks that grew out of folklore.

In Comparison

Like the gun-toting cowboys of the American Wild West, their lore built up over a period of time. For example, if you watch western movies or television shows you often see a pair of cowpokes facing off in the middle of a dusty street. A gawking crowd of gathering onlookers waits for them to draw. After the smoke clears, when one of them lies dead, someone in the crowd might say of the winner, "He sure is quick on the draw".

What's wrong with this scenario? First of all, most gunfights in the old west took place in back alleys, away from the eyes of any crowd or those of an arresting town Marshall. Secondly, many individuals were ambushed from behind then shot in the back with a sawed-off double barrel shotgun rather than some fancy six-shooter. Thirdly, most holsters back in those days were made of flimsy leather and were unsuited for fast draws like you

see in pictures. Some cowboys didn't even own holsters, rather they simply tucked a revolver inside a belted waistline.

So, over a period of more than a century of embellishing storytellers and film makers they created an image of fast draw shootouts. The same is true with the ninja. The author recently watched a documentary where the opening scene shows a one exiting a building and being confronted by a pair of sword-wielding Samurai. The announcer says, "The Samurai are about to die." It gave the viewer the impression that these combatants were the best fighters who ever lived and could take on multiple opponents all at once. In reality, the Samurai likely spent more time practicing with a sword than the ninja, who were busily occupied with the task of developing their espionage skills.

For More Ninja Movie Selections See the Cinema Chapter.

What Made the Shinobi Notorious and Feared?

It was the fact that they learned how to operate in the shadows, or be camouflaged in such a way as to not be seen. Then, waiting patiently for their target to appear, they would leap out from behind and stab them in the back with a sharp tool or else strangle them with a garrote. They would not stand out in the open, face an opponent with a drawn sword, then challenge them to a duel as the cinema often depict. Ruthless skullduggery and hide-and-seek tactics were more their style.

DEFINED

A Definition

"Ninjutsu, or ninpo, is a collection of adaptable survival techniques that allows one to face the uncertainties of life and to respond to dangerous situations, through physical and psychological discipline, where one uses orthodox weapons in unorthodox ways." – Dr. Kacem Zhoughari

What is the difference Between Ninjitsu and Ninjutsu?

The sole difference is in the pronunciation, and how it is written in the Japanese language. Otherwise, they pretty much mean the same thing. But the correct pronunciation of the term "Ninjutsu" often sounds like 'Ninjitsu', and it doesn't have anything to do with it being a fake form or not. If you have the opportunity, then listen when the Japanese people use this word. Plus keep in mind that pronunciation is one of the more difficult things in Japanese.

SCROLLS

Where Did Their Historical Information Originate?

Much of it is found in the Bansenshukai, a Japanese book containing a collection of knowledge from the clans in the Iga and Koga regions that had been devoted to the training of Ninjutsu. It was compiled by Fujibayashi Sabuji in 1676, in the early years of the Tokugawa shogunate, to preserve the knowledge that had been developed during the near-constant military conflict from the Onin War until the end of the Siege of Osaka almost 150 years later.

Along with the Shoninki of 1681 and the Ninpiden of 1655 they make up the three major sources of direct data about this shadowy profession. The Ninpiden (a.k.a. Shinobi Hiden) or Legends of Ninja Secrets is a ninjutsu manual attributed to either Hattori Kiyonobu or Hattori Hanzo. It was passed down in the Hattori family, was considered a secret transmission; not shared with outsiders or even within their kin as few had access to it.

Be aware that none of these documents discuss martial arts. Rather they discuss reconnaissance, news gathering, and similar topics. That is a primary reason why authentic ninjas are thought to be more like informants rather than military style combatants.

THEIR ORIGINS

"We should study our history very carefully, and not just rely on being told the facts told by others".

That was Dr. Masaaki Hatsumi on quoting his instructor Takamatsu sensei, who was also known as Mōoko no Tora (The *Mongolian Tiger*). He is attributed as a martial arts master by members of the Bujinkan organization.

The Beginnings

In the 6th century BC, the Sonbu no heiho contained early Japanese military strategy. It was made up of teachings from the famous Sun Zi, author of the "Art of War" (sixth century BC).

Some historians have claimed that this book may have served as the original ninja manual.

As immigrants began to arrive in Japan from China and Korea, the styles of kenpo (Chinese martial art using bare hands and weapons), and genjutsu (art of illusion and conjuring) were mixed with the local customs of Japan.

Among these immigrants were warrior monks and military personnel that settled in mountainous areas where they met the yamabushi (hermits of the mountains). These mountain hermits, monks, and ascetics used early forms of Ninjutsu.

It was in this time that these yamabushi developed the mysterious and supernatural persona which we know today. Even though they remained separated from society, many senior government officials and warrior families maintained close relationships to these yamabushi who, at times, carried out jobs that needed to be kept secret.

When Did They Exist?

Primarily during Japan's unrest of the Sengoku period (15th to 17th centuries), spies and mercenaries for hire became active in the Iga Province and the adjacent area around the village of Koga, and it is from the area's people that much of our knowledge of the them is drawn. Following the unification of Japan under the Tokugawa shogunate (17th century), they faded into obscurity.

With the introduction of the firearm by the Portuguese in 1540, and an impending Western threat, times had changed culturally and traditional Japanese knowledge and militant tradition gave way to Western manners in industry.

Why Were They Formed?

The first specialized training began during the fifteenth century, when certain samurai families started to focus on covert warfare, which included undercover work and assassination.

Ninjas originated in the mountains of Japan during that time as a form of survival. Mountain dwellers found themselves caught up in the civil wars which raged between warring factions. Hiding out in these hills to practice certain survival methods became a way of life. They soon found themselves hiring out their skills as practitioners of ninjutsu which later became known as "the art of stealth" or "the art of invisibility."

Is Ninjutsu a Real Martial Art?

Ninjutsu and martial arts are two distinct disciplines for historical ninja. They are not the same thing. Ninjutsu is a martial art, while the Shinobijutsu, also known as Ninjitsu, includes military tactics, modus operandi, infiltration, sabotage, intelligence etc.

Foundations

Unlike other martial arts, Ninjutsu has no actual foundation point such a certain date in time, or a particular individual who created it. However, through a deeper understanding of Japanese history, references can be made to help understand Ninjutsu's place in time.

Ninjutsu Is Unique

Ninjutsu is not bujutsu (martial techniques), nor can it be classified as a competition art. Unlike other martial arts where you directly face your opponent and are bound by certain rules while performing a certain set of moves, the Shinobi is like a ghost to the opponent who resorts to unscrupulous tactics. The word "shinobi" is a much better term to find documented references to the ninja as we know it. The Hojo Godai-ki uses other terms such as rappa and seppa, while the Koyo Gunkan uses kagimono-kiki.

In English, ninjutsu means "the art of remaining unseen" or "the invisible art," but to achieve this deceptive persona, one must acquire certain levels of discipline. Deception, in any martial art is a great weapon, and no other art deals with deception better than Ninjutsu. They specialized in evasion and direct, hit-and-run rapid action. It is no wonder why the lords of feudal Japan sought to keep Ninjutsu practitioners on their side during a war.

Keep in mind that fighting arts during certain eras were very inflexible and linear. The armor used in battle by Samurai was heavy and likely limited movement, although the bujutsu at that time included techniques with and without it. As times changed and it wasn't used as much the need for techniques and moves for unarmed combat became crucial.

Were they always called Ninjas?

Ninjutsu is sometimes used interchangeably with the modern term 'ninpo', meaning the strategy and tactics of unconventional warfare, guerrilla warfare and surveillance purportedly practiced by the shinobi (commonly known outside Japan). The word shinobi appears in written records as far back as the late eighth century in poems in the Man'yoshu. Early records show the word shinobi is almost always used.

The word "Ninja" derives from the Japanese characters "nin" and "ja." The term "ninja" didn't appear until the 1800's, long after real ones existed. Prior to that, the word "shinobi" was used, which meant "to sneak" and described a covert agent or condottiere in feudal Japan.

ASSASSINS

Were They Assassins?

Espionage was their chief role. As cloak and dagger artists they spent more time in the spy business rather than in the assassination trade.

While ninjas were trained in covert operations, propaganda, and observation they only acted as assassins in secondary roles. Their manuals rarely discuss the subject.

How Did They Operate?

They were not necessarily independent or self-serving, but often hired themselves out for brutish service to a particular Daimyo (feudal lord).

Unlike exuberant action flicks, in the act of surveillance, observing and scouting sought to avoid open battlefield combat, especially when faced with numerically superior enemy forces. Hence their style was adapted to cloak and dagger methods, or to stun the enemy with hit-and-run tactics.

SECRETS

How Secretive Were they?

There was more written about Samurai history than that of these warriors. This may be due to the fact that anyone caught by the enemy in the act of subterfuge could face a death sentence. Therefore, it is likely that they would have been cautious about jotting down activities or keeping diaries.

As mountain dwellers or farmers, they trained mostly in secret, deep in the forest hills away from common villages. The laws of Ninjutsu forbade them to reveal to anyone they were or to use Ninjutsu for their own benefit or reward. Should they break the laws and reveal their secrets they could be slain by members of their own group.

Did They Have Secret Identities?

They were divided into those who could be seen and those who remain hidden. The hidden ones were those whose identity was kept secret so that they could move out on missions without anyone knowing who they were.

On the other hand, a number of them would be hired in the open. They moved with an army, had their own barracks, were exempt from day time camp duties and were well known among their peers. In the later years of peace, they even had their own jacket and crest that they wore around the castle.

Did They Use Disguises?

Ninjas were particularly adept at traveling in incognito in the ancient writings of the Buke Myomokusho it states, "Shinobi-monomi (ninja) were people used in secret ways, and their duties were to go into the mountains and pass themselves off as firewood gatherers to discover and acquire the news about an enemy's territory."

As intelligence agents, they not only would commonly use various disguises but also adopt an alias to blend into the landscape. They might take on roles such as that of a farmer, landscaper, craftsman, magician, poet, artist, juggler, carpenter, beggar, priest, musician, fortune teller, merchant, or monk.

Or perhaps they took on the role of a ronin ("drifter" or "wanderer"), which was a Samurai without lord or master during the feudal period of Japan. A Samurai became master-less from the demise of his lord or after the loss of his overlord's favor or privilege.

UNIFORMS

Did They Wear Masks?

There are no references to them wearing masks anywhere in history, including the ancient scrolls. Supposedly, they resorted to covering their faces with their long sleeves when the enemy was near, and when working in groups they wore white headbands so they could see each other in the moonlight.

In early Japan, male and female alike wore a head scarf on colder days. Such covering could be where the infamous ninja hood legend originated and grew out of proportion.

What was fascinating about the so-called ninja scarf (or zukin hood) was that it was longer than traditional and reported to be multi-functional. It could be used as an emergency rope for climbing, to filter drinking water from a murky pond, as a tourniquet or bandage, to tie up a victim, or as a makeshift weapon by inserting a rock in the center, then by gripping the loose ends swung as a club. **See Illustration #1**

Did They Wear Black?

While the image of them clad in black garb (shinobi shozoku) is prevalent in popular media, there is no written evidence for a black costume. Instead, it was much more common for the ninja to be made inconspicuous as civilians.

A popular argument is that they did not wear black but rather wore brown to blend in more with common surroundings of nature. Still, others say that in villages they wore blue as this color originated from a manual called the Shoninki (True Path of the Ninja) written in 1681. It stated that they should wear blue to blend in with crowds as this color was popular, meaning that they would not stand out if people were looking for them. **See Illustration #1**

ILLUSTRATION #1

In the book NINJA ATTACK (Tuttle publishing) Matt Alt and co-author Hiroko Yoda examine the written aspect. "A Fifteenth Century ninja would laugh out loud at the sight of a dude in black pajamas running around a modern city. The whole point of a ninja was to blend in." That is why they often dressed as farmers so they could do just that as they collected information and scouted enemies.

Where Did the Black Outfit Concept Originate?

Historian Stephen Turnbull suggested that the stereotypical image of ones dressed all in black derived from kabuki. The Kuroko are stage hands in traditional Japanese theater, who dress all in black. In kabuki theater, the they move scenery and props on stage, aiding in scene changes and costume changes. They wore all black, from head to toe, in order to imply that they are invisible and not part of the action on stage. The practice of wearing black is a central element in bunraku puppet theater as well.

There are no historical chronicles that suggests that they had a certain uniform like you see today in cinema and art. Most likely they wore the common Japanese clothing of the day, and that meant whatever was comfortable or appropriate for field use or while walking thru villages.

As stated earlier, they might use a camouflage when walking among the enemy, and/or certain clothes with solid footwear when performing night raids along with lighter less restricting attire when infiltrating houses, none of which would have required a mask.

MARTIAL ARTS

Were They Expert Martial Artists?

Since their primary function was the act of espionage, hand-to-hand combat would have been a secondary skill. It's been said, "A successful ninja is one who never fights", meaning that fighting should only be used as a last resort. There is also an old saying, "Ye who runs away today shall live to fight another day." While that statement is not linked to them, it sounds like it could be linked to their hit-and-run tactics.

But if they did practice self-defense, then what style would they use? Before there was our common Judo, Karate, and Jiujutsu which are popular today, many believe there was an earlier form of Jujutsu which featured more of the older approaches such as lethal throws and brutal joint locks.

And since a common opponent of the ninja could be a samurai employed by the opposition who was decked out in tough armor, hammering away at that with one's fists does not seem like a good idea. Therefore, moves that could knock that type of soldier off their feet in order to neutralize them might seem the most practical.

Because of this, some researchers have suggested that the martial art style of them may have been known as Aiki-jujutsu. Originally called Daitō-ryū jujitsu, its origins and supposed lineage extend back approximately nine hundred years.

In modern day, one of its best-known students was Morihei Ueshiba, who later became the founder of Aikido. Modern Japanese jujutsu and aikido both originated in aiki-jujutsu, which emphasizes "an early neutralization of an attack". Like other forms of jujutsu, it emphasizes throwing styles and joint manipulations to effectively subdue or injure an attacker. Of particular importance is the timing of a defensive technique either to blend with or to neutralize an attack's effectiveness and to use the force of the attacker's advances against him.

Jujutsu as we know it today however, tends to be a generalized term for wrestling/grappling, and is more of a sport theme often tied to activities such mixed martial arts (MMA).

Taijutsu, while commonly associated with Ninjas today, it is essentially a Japanese blanket term for any combat skill, procedure or system of martial art using body movements that are described as an empty-hand combat skill or system.

Which Martial Arts Did the Ninja Practice?

The ninja excelled in all the martial arts of their day, such as kendo, kyudo and naginata-do. They were also skilled in hand-to-hand combat, using wrestling and boxing techniques that were the forerunners of judo and karate.

SWORDS

Did They Use Samurai Swords?

Only actual Samurai were privileged to carry them. It was highly illegal for anyone to own or carry an authentic Katana sword unless you were an actual Samurai. **See Illustration #2**

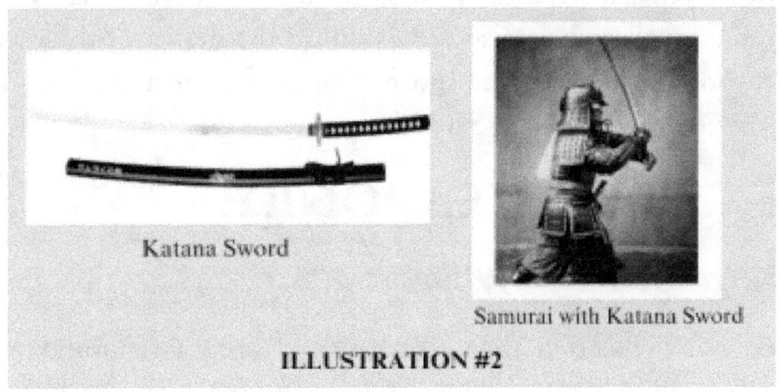

To the Samurai, the sword was his right hand, a family heirloom, and soul. Being that it was a work of art, a badge of honor and class distinction, the sword was such a valuable piece of equipment it was not available to the general public.

If a one stole a Samurai sword, or came into possession of one for personal use, that would be the equivalent of impersonating a police officer of which he (or she) might be sentenced to death.

What Type of Sword Would They Use?

Supposedly they were straight bladed, unlike the curved Samurai blades. This made them easier to manufacture. Many of their swords were crafted in mountain villages and likely crude in comparison to the exquisite and sacred versions used by the Samurai.

Others suggest a sword carried by the them was the shinobigatana. This sword was shorter and preferred to be carried across the back (rather than in a waist sash like the Samurai) with the hilt sticking out above the right shoulder. This was to make it easier for them to climb trees or scale walls without the sword getting in the way.

Still, others will debate this. There is no actual physical evidence for the existence of this so-called "katana-like short sword" legendarily used by ninja before the Twentieth Century. Though it is believed that the designs demonstrated by alleged replicas are based on the design of the wakizashi or chokuto swords, which was the shorter companion to the famed katana or secondary sword carried by the Samurai.

WEAPONRY

Was the Sword Their Primary Weapon?

If their goal was to blend in, then utilizing or adapting agricultural implements as weapons would be far more logical while working incognito. A broomstick could be a staff, a flail was a threshing tool, and a chain with a weight attached to the end could become a kusari-fundo. **See Illustration #3**

The Logical Weapon

Since many would pass themselves off as farmers the primary weapon of choice was not a sword, another option (and more likely choice) would be the kusarigama, which was a sickle with a lengthy weighted chain attached. The chain was swung to injure, snag, or trip an opponent, and the sickle was then used to slay at close range. This weapon was ideal because it could be easily dissembled into common tools. **See Illustration #3**

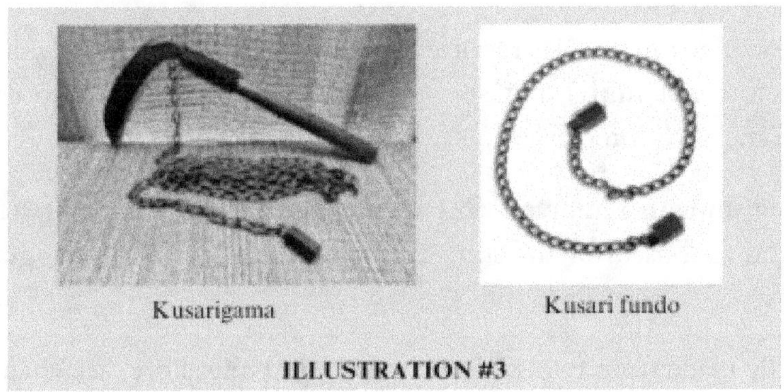

ILLUSTRATION #3

Did They Use Nunchakus?

Wood-handled nunchakus, made famous by the legendary Bruce Lee, were not known to be common battlefield weapons because they were considered ineffective against long armament such as swords and spears. **See Illustration #4.**

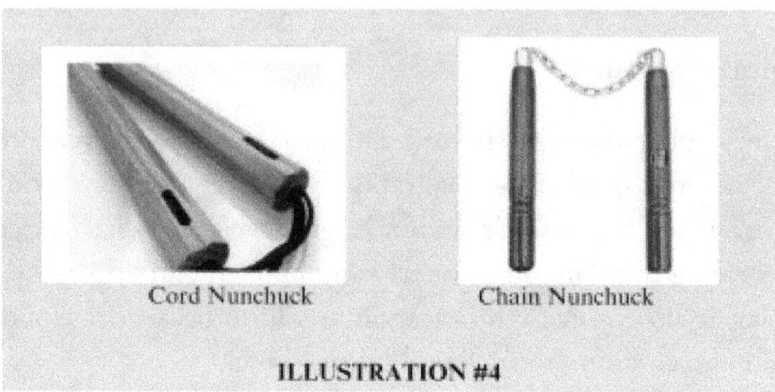

Cord Nunchuck   Chain Nunchuck

ILLUSTRATION #4

Not only was the nunchaku reported to be Okinawan in origin (not Japanese and therefore not ninja), but so were tonfa and sai, which also commonly appear in their motion pictures.

The closest thing to a nunchuk that they might have used is a flail, which is an agricultural tool used for threshing and the process of separating grains from their husks.

It is usually made from two sticks (one long and one short) attached together by a short chain or cord. The longer pole is held and swung, causing the shorter one to strike a pile of grain, loosening the husks.

The flail is proposed as a possible origin of the shorter two-piece baton known in the Okinawan kobudō weapon system as the nunchaku.

Did They Use Throwing Stars?

Sharp-pointed throwing stars were a weapon used in various Samurai schools and they only became linked to the them in the Twentieth Century through movies, comic books, and animation. **See Illustration #5**

Furthermore, in all the shinobi documents left behind only one "Ninja throwing star" is ever mentioned and even then, it's in reference to shinobi working in peacetime to apprehend criminals.

Action films love to portray throwing stars as deadly slayers. But in reality, unless they struck a vital body part or were poison-coated they were usually too small and light to slay someone with ease. Their principal value was to distract, slow down, or injure an opponent, like during an escape.

Throwing Weapons

A knife or spike could have been a possibility during that period. These were concealable and said to be used by Samurai.

Easier to craft than a throwing star were throwing spikes, which were simple slender metal shafts sharpened at the tip that could range in length from five inches on up to a foot. **See Illustration #5**

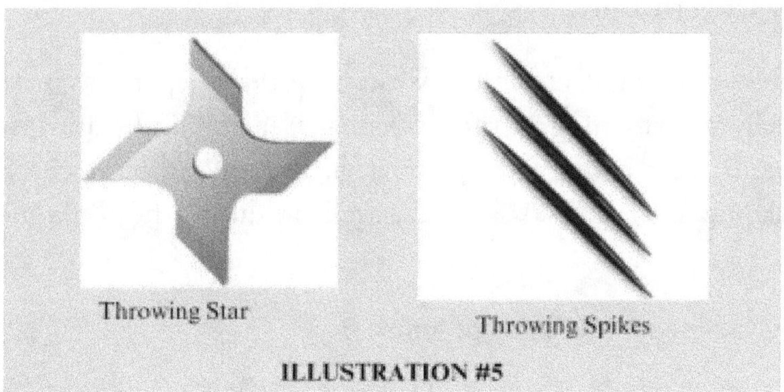

ILLUSTRATION #5

Their Resourcefulness

They were highly resourceful woodsmen, and did not necessarily require specialized gear. Nature itself could supply various tools or weapons simply by applying one's craftsmanship and imagination.

For instance, in outdoor regions tree branches could easily become a club, staff, or spear. Ordinary rocks could become a tool for throwing or bashing. When a handle is attached to a stone you now have a lethal club or axe. Attach a rock to a rope and which made a bola. If you have some cord then bow and arrow could be easily crafted. Hollow bamboo could serve as a blowgun for wooden darts. A handful of dirt or sand thrown into the eyes could temporarily blind an opponent and thus enable victory or escape.

GUNPOWDER

Did They Use Explosives?

Arson was the primary form of sabotage practiced by them, who targeted castles and camps. Explosives introduced from China, however, were known in Japan by the time of the Mongol Invasions in the thirteenth century.

Designs for hand-held bombs, grenades, fragmentation explosives, and soft-cased bombs designed to release poison gas appear in their manuals. How well they functioned, or how widely they were used, is unknown.

Did They Use Firearms?

The introduction of guns from the Western world to Japan was in 1543. They would likely use anything to their advantage, including firearms, when they could obtain them along with gunpowder. Primitive matchlock or flintlock style black powder muzzle loaders were available during the Ninja and Samurai periods.

Did They Escape with Clouds of Smoke?

In popular films shows a ninja could easily escape his surrounding captors by employing a thick cloud of smoke, then miraculously vanishing from sight into thin air. The image of them using a golf ball sized smoke bomb is universal, but misleading. Ancient manuals do not contain smoke bombs but they do contain recipes for various fire tools such as land mines, grenades, waterproof torches, forms of Greek fire, fire arrows, explosives, and poisonous gas.

TRAINING

Did They Train from Childhood?

According to Stephen Turnbull, they trained from childhood, which was also a common discipline among Samurai families.

Researchers have also suggested that running, jumping, and climbing events were often encouraged by parents and concealed as games.

Strength, endurance, and balance were aided by hanging from tree limbs, standing on one leg for long periods, plus walking across logs suspended off the ground. Training while blindfolded developed other senses such as hearing and also simulated night work for operating in the dark.

Outside the expected martial art disciplines, training for reconnaissance, tactics included wilderness survival (living off the land), scouting techniques, a crafty style of moving silently and camouflage, as well as information regarding poisons, first aid, and explosives.

Were they World Class Athletes?

They are often portrayed as Olympic-caliber acrobats who perform dazzling feats. But as most of their life was spent in forests, and with the necessity of moving over difficult terrain, physical skills such as long-distance hiking, climbing, and swimming would be required for scouting.

HONOR

Did They hold to Certain Ideals like the Noble Samurai?

The Samurai code of conduct, known as Bushido, held that the true warrior must hold loyalty, courage, veracity, compassion, and honor as important, above all else.

In regards to the ninja, however, their covert methods of waging irregular warfare were deemed dishonorable and beneath the Samurai-caste, who observed strict rules about honor and combat.

As a result, they were both hired and feared as diabolical humans, although they were almost invariably despised because of the contrast their ways presented to the Samurai code of behavior. This may be partly due to the fact that many had their origins in the lower social classes, and that their secretive and underhand approach was the exact opposite of the ideals of the noble Samurai.

These combatants represent the dark side in the world of the Samurai. In contrast to the image of the noble, fearless soldier facing squarely on to his worthy opponent with drawn sword, the ninja is a creature of darkness and stealth, whose craft is guile, cunning, treachery, and murder. One who would stoop to any measure in order to win.

I've heard it said, "If ninjas were around today, they would be classified as criminals or terrorists.

Were the Samurai and Ninja Enemies?

Film likes to portray them as hateful opponents. In truth, often they teamed up, depending on which side daimyo (feudal lords) they were on. Ninja groups sometimes fought with one another in attempts to create or destroy emperors. The need for spies and informants grew as these families dueled for supremacy.

Many were known to be suspicious or jealous of one another and would resort to any means necessary to eliminate possible threats. Therefore, practitioners of clandestine operations were in great demand. With this, the true Ninja was born.

LABELS

Who Wore the Label of a Ninja?

Anyone may be recruited as an informant in order to perform an act of espionage or destruction, given sufficient incentives, either of financial reward or by threat of bodily harm. It could be an individual of any age, male or female, and even someone with no special training or particular background.

Amateurs caught in the act of spying or sabotage risked being charged and sentenced whether they belonged to a clan or not.

Were There Female Ninja?

Female ninjas, known as kunoichi, formed an important part of medieval shinobi clans. Like their male counterparts, these women trained in combat, disguise, and cunning. Their missions and function, however, differed from those of male counterparts in several important ways.

Most Westerners think of ninjas as black-masked men with swords who appear from the shadows and strike without warning. But not all where assassins nor were they male, and not all of them walked in the shadows.

Samurai, a dominant force during that period, rarely trusted strangers, but often made exceptions for women, either because of their beauty or because the woman filled a "harmless" social role. By contrast, a kunoichi could gain her target's trust until he allowed her intimate access, at which point she could attack when his guard were down.

The kunoichi were known to train with a variety of weapons. Most knew how to use a sword, though they usually specialized in a certain type of close quarter hand-to-hand combat. They had a preference for daggers, garrotes, poisons, and specialty items like bladed fans (tessen) and poison laden claw-like finger extensions known as neko-te. **See Illustration #6**

Kunoichi: Female Ninja   Tessen: Weapon Fan

ILLUSTRATION #6

But kunoichi didn't sneak around under the cover of darkness and they rarely slayed their targets right away.

She would take her time, earning the target's trust and often becoming a part of his household (like working as a mistress, maid, or servant). From that trusted position, she passed this knowledge on to his enemies or struck when he let his defenses down.

In these disguises, kunoichi infiltrated temples, castles, and fortresses, either to gather information or to strike at well-protected targets male assassins could not reach.

While researching the archives they do state there are no records that female kunoichi existed, meaning those which contend female were similarly active as their male counterparts. However, that does not mean they didn't perform certain tasks of high importance for the ninja.

Often the cinema depicts women as maids who spied on employers, or else female assassins who worked as seducers who, upon luring their male victims, employed hidden hairpins tipped with poison.

Kunoichi, is, originally, an argot or slang which means "woman", it supposedly came from the characters (pronounced ku, no and ichi), which make up the three strokes that form the kanji for "woman". In stories written in the modern era, Kunoichi means "female ninja".

OCCULT

Ninjutsu and the Occult

There are reports that Ninjutsu has roots in the occult by practitioners who summoned up demonic powers thru spiritualism or contacting other worldly forces by various means. Exactly how they went about this, and what portion of the community was involved, is unclear. But their goal was to gain personal power in order to accomplish them, and would resort to any means necessary, even if that meant unworldly assistance.

In today's world, Church leaders state that those who dabble in spiritualism engage in activities that seem innocuous or harmless but they could actually open the door for demonic contact, harassment and even possession.

Many followers of spiritualism in the modern world are on record as having been traumatized and harmed psychologically, if not physically, by contacts with demons that began with seances, Ouija boards, psychic consultations, contacting wizards, palm reading and encounters with mediums.

What Are the Principal Dangers of Spiritualism?

In addition to psychological problems, physical troubles of various kinds have been known to occur such as stomach pains, pains in the forehead and bones, vomiting, epileptic fits, pins and needles in the legs, sudden attacks of heat or cold, increasing sense of anxiety, depression, constant nervous tics, or inability to take in food.

Along with the inability to sleep night or day, failure to study or work. To be agitated, have nightmares, to be afraid of the dark, to have the sensation of being grabbed by the arms, or the sensation of someone sitting on our lap. One could also feel invisible slaps and bites, as well as blows to the body.

As the author of this book is a Christian himself, and as one who has spent time studying demonic possession and believes it to be real, based on case studies, he must close this topic by quoting Jesus from the Holy Bible verse John 14:6, "I am the way and the truth and the life. No one comes to the Father except through me."

MAGIC

Were They Capable of Mystical and Magical Feats?

Incredible feats such as walking on water, walking thru walls, shape shifting, and even disappearing into thin air are all part of the ninja legend.

According to Stephen Turnball, "I personally do not think they had any success in the notion that the ninja had any particular mystic powers. It was one of the myths that they encouraged to make people more frightened of them."

Today we refer to similar actions as wise psychological warfare, which is defined in the dictionary as, "The use of propaganda, threats, and other psychological methods to mislead, intimidate, demoralize, or otherwise influence the thinking or behavior of an opponent."

Legendary Myths

Their adaption of kites in warfare is another subject of legend, such as them being lifted into the air by kites, where they flew over hostile terrain and descended into, or dropped bombs on enemy territory. Kites were indeed used in Japanese warfare, but mostly for the purpose of sending messages and relaying signals.

Chronicler Stephen Turnbull suggests that kites lifting a man into midair might have been technically feasible, but states that the use of kites to form a human "hang glider" falls squarely in the realm of fantasy.

LEGENDS

Myth Busters

According to Television's pop science show 'Myth Busters' that aired on the Discovery channel, it starred special effects experts Adam Savage and Jamie Hyneman who used their expertise to test the validity of various rumors and urban legends. They busted the following three myths regarding Ninjas, and their results are printed below:

Episode 78: Walking on Water

(1) Did They Have the Ability to Run Across Water?

To test this myth, Adam tried various special shoe designs, including Mizugumo, which were meant to increase his surface area on the water or increase his buoyancy. However, the shoes either failed to keep Adam afloat or made too much noise as he tried to cross the body of water. Jamie then created a non-Newtonian fluid from a mixture of water and corn starch, which made the water solid enough for Adam to run across unaided. However, it is unlikely that they had access to large amounts of corn starch, so the myth was busted.

(2) Could They Catch Arrows in Midair?

To start off, Jamie fired arrows blunted with tennis balls while Adam tried to catch them. Though it took several tries, Adam did manage to catch the arrows flying through the air. However, these arrows were only moving at a third of the speed as a normal arrow. In order to test a full speed arrow, Adam and Jamie built an artificial hand that could close with both human and superhuman speed. The artificial hand managed to catch the arrow easily at that pace, but the human strength setting was just not effective enough to grip the arrow in time.

(3) Could They Catch a Sword Between Their Bare Palms?

To test this myth, the build team constructed a machine to swing a sword as well as a pair of artificial hands to try and catch it. However, during their tests, the hands were simply not fast enough to catch the sword, plus they suffered damage as they attempted to stop the blade. When they consulted an expert, he pointed out that it would be more prudent to either block or dodge the sword rather than trying to catch it with your bare palms. He did show that with the use of Ninja Shuko Climbing Claws, he could easily block a sword with a single hand.

(4) Blowgun Test

The crew at Myth Busters also ran another test to see if one could hide underwater by employing a blowgun as a snorkel. Then, while rising up out of the water use the blowgun to accurately strike a target with a dart. And yes, they did confirm that such tactics are plausible.

CLANS

What Were Ninja Clans?

The plains of Iga, nested in secluded mountains, gave rise to villages specialized in their training. The Iga and Koga people have come to describe families living in the province of Iga (modern Mie Prefecture) and the adjacent region of Koka (later written as Koga), named after a village in what is now Shiga Prefecture. From these regions, villages devoted to the training of Ninja originated.

Such remoteness and inaccessibility of the surrounding mountains are thought to play a role in the secretive development of the shinobi. Writings regarding their origins in these mountainous regions are considered generally correct.

A distinction should be pointed out between the Ninja from these areas, and commoners or Samurai hired as spies or mercenaries. Unlike their counterparts, the Iga and Koga families produced professional ninja, specifically trained for their combatant roles.

Were They from the Peasant Class?

Popular media also portrays the Ninja to be from the peasant class. In truth, they could be from any class, either Samurai or non-Samurai. It was only after 1600 when peace spread over Japan that the official position of ninja inside a clan was reduced from full Samurai to a new social position called doshin, or half Samurai. As time progressed the ninja became lower in status, however they still held a higher social position than most peasants.

It should be mentioned that the two most famous "Ninjas" in history, Hattori Hanzo and Yagyuu Jubei, were both Samurai.

Could Outsiders Join a Ninja Clan?

Like the Samurai, Shinobi were born into the profession, where traditions were kept in, and passed down through the family. Outsiders were not trusted. Therefore, one must be born into a family, many of which were scattered throughout the mountainous regions of Japan. The only exception was an orphaned infant that was adopted by them.

The Fuma Clan

These legendary groups were one of the smaller bands that operated out of Kanagawa. While the Iga and Koga lineage mostly did not take part in direct combat, in preference to assassination, spy craft, and sabotage, the Fuma were horse mounted guerrilla fighters.

The Fumas would ride in with a small, highly trained horse mounted force, attack the enemy at its weakest point and then fade away before reinforcements could be called to the scene. Not only did they practice these mounted ambushes, they also used the sea. They could also pull off effective marine, and amphibious attacks (much like pirates!).

Fuma Kotaro

According to the Hojo-Godaiki, Fuma Kotaro was the fifth and the best known of the Fuma leaders. The name of Fuma Kotaro is actually a title, bestowed on the leader of the faction. When a new leader was chosen, he would give up his old name and take upon himself the title of Fuma Kotaro.

Born in Sagami Province (modern Kanagawa Prefecture) on an unknown date, he became notorious as the leader of a band of two hundred Rappa "battle disrupters" based in Kanagawa Prefecture.

His biggest achievement came in 1580, when the Fuma ninja covertly infiltrated and attacked a camp of the Takeda gang forces under Takeda Katsuyori at night, succeeding in causing severe chaos in the camp, which resulted in mass fratricide among the disoriented enemies.

In 1590, Toyotomi Hideyoshi laid siege to Odawara Castle, which eventually fell, and the Hojo tribe was forced to surrender. When the Tokugawa shogunate came to supremacy, the remnants of Fuma-ryu were reduced to a band of brigands operating in and around Edo.

A popular but fictional story claimed that in 1596, Kotaro was responsible for the death of Hattori Hanzo, a famous samurai in the service of Tokugawa Ieyasu. The legend said that Kotaro had tracked Hanzo down in the Inland Sea.

CAPTURE

Note: The act of suicide was also known as Hara Kiri or seppuku.

Would One Kill Himself if he Failed a Mission?

Another Hollywood myth. There is no evidence to show that failure in a mission led to suicide. In fact, some manuals teach that it is better to fail the mission than do it with haste and cause problems. In other words, it was better to wait for another opportunity.

What Happens to One Caught in the Act of Espionage?

Ninjas were reputed for being boiled in oil, a most torturous death that was intended to send a chilling warning to another ninja others. Such barbarous treatment helped to make it a common practice for Ninja to kill themselves when capture was imminent by taking virulent poisons or stabbing themselves with their own blades.

In the event of capture, ninja they were also known to disfigure their faces with a blade in such a way so that they might not be recognized and the source of their ninjutsu traced in order to protect their kin.

Fearing torture, a ninja who had been bound by captors could take his own life by biting harshly thru his own tongue, thus producing a fatal hemorrhage.

TOOLS

Tools of the Ninja

Devices used for infiltration and undercover work remain as some of the most intriguing artifacts related to them, and are on display in the Ninja Museum of Japan.

Examples include simple gardening instruments such as kunai (a heavy pointed tool used for gouging holes in walls) and sickles. Such tools were used as weaponry so that, if discovered, a ninja could claim they are his tools and not weapons, despite their usefulness in battles.

Other examples include various knives, small saws, ropes and grappling hooks, collapsible ladder, cane swords, blowguns, poisoned darts, spiked or hooked climbing gear worn on the hands and feet, chisels, hammers, drills, picks, quick-strike fire tools, and eggshells which could be filled with blinding powder.

While museums can be quite fascinating and draw many gawking visitors from around the globe, they don't necessarily paint an accurate picture of the true ninja by offering much detail regarding their actual history. Instead, they seem designed to draw curious tourists, who may or may not care much about actual facts as long as they feel entertained and get their monies worth. Divided into three segments, there are choreographed demonstrations by armed combatants, a house with hidden trap doors and passages, and a room featuring artifacts that were supposedly used by the shinobi.

Bamboo Canes

An ordinary cane or simple walking stick was popular and could blend in well among the commoners of society and not draw much attention. Yet it could easily be employed as a weapon, as well as a versatile tool. Hollow bamboo shafts were ideal for concealing blades, chains, various powders, maps, and secret messages. They could also be used as blowguns which could fire poison tipped darts.

Bow and Arrow

Despite various depictions were not known to use crossbows. Nor did they use longer precision bows like that of the Samurai or the English and their famed long bows. A bow was generally crude in design and shorter in length for compact carry and climbing chores.

The fact that it was smaller meant it was less effective and intended mostly for close range usage. When not serving as a potential weapon it could be used with flaming arrows to send a signal or to set an opponent's structure ablaze.

Climbing Claws

They are noted for climbing trees and scaling certain types of walls that would stop most people. This was due to a set of metal claws called shinobi shuko. Traditionally, they consisted of metal or leather bands which slipped over their hands, with a set of metal spikes that protruded forward from the wearer's palm. The ease and speed with which a shuko-wearing shinobi could scale a tree or wall added to the legends surrounding their amazing skills. **See Illustration #7**

Like many of their weapons, the shuko were multi-functional. The claws gave the wearer a solid grip when climbing, and also served as a weapon in hand-to-hand combat. It could be also be used to help block the strike of a sword blade or spear thrust.

They also used spiked foot bands to complement shuko to aid with climbing. Such bands worn on the feet were called ashiko, and were usually designed to slip on over shoes or other footwear. In some cases, they were designed with thongs that slipped between the wearer's big toe and second toe (much like the thong on modern-day flip-flops) to help hold the spiked foot bands in place. **See Illustration #7**

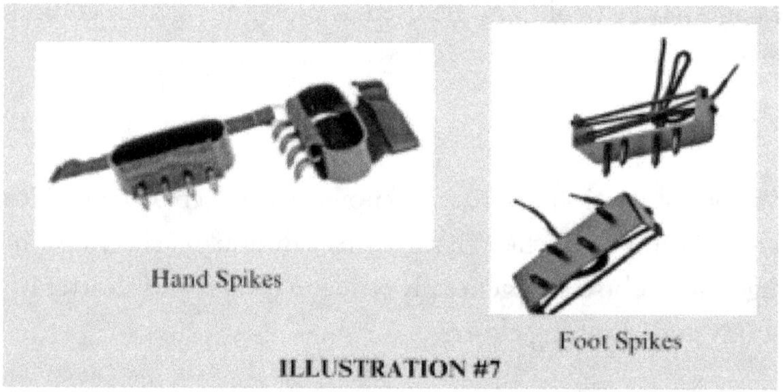

ILLUSTRATION #7

While many popular myths and legends about them are untrue, their skill at scaling up trees or certain types of walls, however, is one that has its root in truth. With the aid of shuko (and ashiko), Japanese ninjas really could scale trees or certain walls much faster than most people can imagine. Proof of this is visible if you've ever seen a telephone repairman scale up a wooden phone pole with their specialized foot spikes, waist belts, and gloves.

Kaginawa

This is a type of grappling hook used as a tool in feudal Japan by the samurai class, their retainers, foot soldiers and reportedly by ninja. Kaginawa is the combination of the words kagi meaning hook and nawa meaning rope. They have several configurations, from one to four hooks.

The kagi would be attached to a nawa of varying length; this was then used to scale a rather large wall, to secure a boat, or for hanging up armor and other equipment during the night. Kaginawa were regularly used during various sieges of miscellaneous castles. The nawa was attached to a ring on one end which could be used to hang it from a saddle. **See Illustration #8**

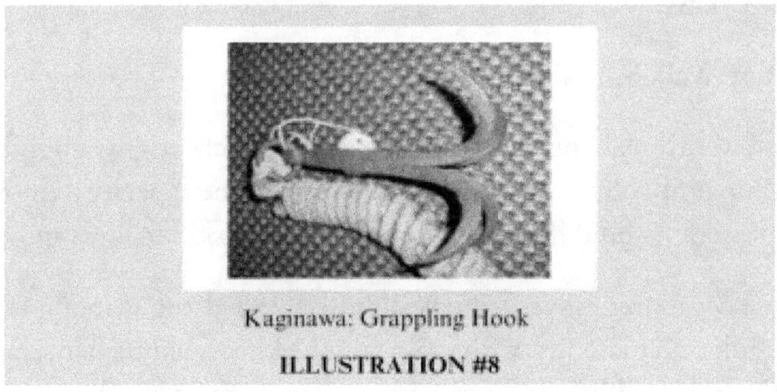

Kaginawa: Grappling Hook
ILLUSTRATION #8

Versatility for Success

Despite the large array of accessories available to them, the Bansenshukai scroll warns one not to be overburdened with equipment by stating, "A successful Ninja is one who uses but one tool for multiple tasks".

SKILLS

What Other Skills Were Associated with Them?

Field craft and survival approaches included camouflage, herbal medicine, weather forecasting, poisons, edible plants, star navigation, controlled breathing, agriculture, ways to avoid detection, methods of escape, how to draw a map, how to purify water, cooking rice in camp by wrapping it in a wet cloth and burying it underneath a small campfire.

Are They Famous for Secret Hand Gestures?

Known as kuji by the Japanese, it has no real connection to them. Kuji was reportedly started in India then moved to China before making its way into Japan.

It is a series of specific hand gestures with bold claims of sharpening the mind, reducing stress, warding off evil, bolstering courage or aiding endurance in certain situations.

Could They Walk Silently Without Detection?

A form of stealth walking actually did exist, yet such origins might be traced back to China's Shaolin monk warriors. No doubt, the capacity to move silently without detection could have been a useful survival skill to any type of soldier.

The primary walking moves supposedly used, called the shinobi-ashi, was to walk carefully and patiently, with poise and the knees slightly bent; first placing the fourth, then middle toe on the ground and smoothly rolling down to the heel. This was a valuable asset when time was not limited, as the gentle and flowing nature of the foot in a rolling motion allowed almost silent movement.

Discipline

Not only must shinobi learn to maneuver quietly in enemy territory, but how to stand perfectly still in the shadows for long periods without detection. Equally important was how to tolerate discomforts in uncomfortable situations such as thirst, hunger, and tolerating bad weather conditions.

What are the Five Elements?

Everything in nature is said to be made up of five basic elements: earth, water, fire, air, and space. Supposedly, knowledge of the five elements allows the user to understand the laws of nature and to attain greater health, power, knowledge, wisdom, and happiness.

While some have attributed this to being utilized by the ninja, there is no documentation verifying this. The knowledge of the five elements originated out of India and yoga. Historians say it was likely added to the lists of techniques at a later time, rather than during their heyday.

What Foods did They Eat?

They would use anything to their advantage, which might include dietary information as well. It was known at the time that the avoidance of meat, fish, dairy foods, and sugars in favor of a diet centered on whole-grain brown rice, tofu, and vegetables was not only better for health reasons, but made an individual lighter on their feet when they were forced to move quickly. Also, to avoid being detected when sneaking or hiding, they might avoid foods that could lead to body odor and bad breath.

ESPIONAGE

Did They Invent Secret Warfare?

Secret warfare was not an isolated Japanese specialty, nor was it confined to the Sengoku Period. Undercover operations are to be found throughout the Japanese past, and one component of their modern cult has been to exaggerate this fact by crediting certain noted figures with being ninja or 'proto-ninja'.

Counterintelligence tactics do not belong exclusively to them. Nearly all pre-modern cultures have spies and saboteurs. Events involving covert actions are well chronicled.

For an example dating way back in time, the Old Testament of the Christian Bible, which is based primarily on the Hebrew Bible, speaks about Joshua and Caleb and the twelve spies when entering the Promised Land.

The ancient writings of Chinese and Indian military strategists such as Sun-Tzu, (author of The Art of War from the 5th century BC), and Chanakya contain data on deception and subversion. As mentioned earlier, such writings may have served as primary guidelines which influenced the fifteenth century ninja of Japan.

SCHOOLS

Was Earning a Black Belt a Goal?

There was no belt ranking system in ninjutsu like there are in other current forms of martial arts such as karate or judo. Nor were martial arts featured as a competition sport among combatants.

The main goals of these combatants were to accomplish his wartime tasks, whatever they may be, and to survive his constant life and death struggles. Today, however, certain ninja schools do offer various promotions to its students.

Do Schools of Today Teach Authentic Techniques?

Modern schools that claim to teach authentic ninjutsu arose from the craze of the 1970's. The lineage and authenticity of these schools are a matter of much controversy.

A majority of these classes teach martial art close quarter combat drills (hand-to-hand combat and sword skills) are practiced indoors at a dojo (training hall) rather than deception tactics practiced in the wilderness of the great outdoors.

According to noted author and martial arts instructor Stephen K. Hayes, "Finding a master of the dark art of ninjutsu in modern westernized Japan seems as unlikely as finding an active practitioner of the magic of Merlin in contemporary industrialized England."

NINJAS TODAY

Japan's era of shoguns and samurai is long over, but the country does have one, or maybe two, so-called authentic surviving ninjas. Though not without controversy, these are said to be experts in the dark arts of subterfuge and silent ninjas skills that were passed down thru time, like from father to son.

The creator of modern day Ninjutsu is said to be Dr. Masaaki Hatsumi, who is also a chiropractor. There is, however, some controversy regarding his ninja lineage and the formulas he teaches. But he shrugs it off. As far as the martial arts world is concerned, he is the grandfather of Ninjutsu. Many people from all over the world have made the pilgrimage to his dojo in Japan, under the assumption that they are learning authentic techniques from a true master.

Dr. Hatsumi claims his martial arts career began in a very dramatic way. His father was an alcoholic who, often in drunken stupors, brandished a knife at home. As a young boy, he was forced to hide from his drunken father. By listening to the rhythm of his father's footsteps, the boy recognized the drunkenness before his father entered the house. As Hatsumi got older, he learned Ninjutsu and other martial arts to control his father before putting him to bed.

Dr. Hatsumi's Ninjutsu teacher was Toshitsugu Takamatsu, an individual who had spent many years in China learning martial arts. His sheer prowess earned him the nickname Mongolian Tiger. Takamatsu lived to be an old man, and he attributed his longevity to transforming himself from a Mongolian tiger to a house cat.

Want to Become a Real Ninja?

If so, you might be better off joining the military or an intelligence agency like the CIA rather than studying at an indoor martial arts dojo. In today's world, special forces units, commandos, black operatives' personnel are performing similar roles as a they did back in their day.

In the world of spies the main difference is that times have obviously changed greatly, and modern electronic technology and surveillance equipment has become the primary tool. In an age of high-tech firearms and explosives the ancient primitive weapons such as swords and nun chucks seem rather antiquated.

FACT VS. FICTION

Why the Fascination with Ninjas?

Because anyone who studies martial arts then dresses up in a black uniform and possesses a sword can call themselves a ninja, by which they can live out a fantasy of being some type of special or unique individual.

In this fantasy, actual super powers such as incredible strength, ability to fly, invisibility, or firing lightning bolts out of your fingertips, is not required. From an early age, children learn to play 'make believe' which is groomed thru cinema, comic books, and computer games, even though the fantasy is unreal and exists only in the mind.

Today, people might call themselves a ninja for doing almost anything well, from performing extensively in sports, to surviving a gruesome obstacle course.

While the original methods used by these militants were looked down upon and considered dishonorable by the higher caste (the samurai), they were so fascinating and frequently discussed that over centuries of time their exploits became exaggerated by grand storytellers who helped them gain mythological status.

It's similar in the way that people tend to admire gangsters and outlaws, from Al Capone to Billy the Kid. And perhaps that is a sad reflection on the human minds of society, the issue of admiring criminals and even treating such villainous individuals as heroes.

Why Such Confusion Over the Facts?

Why is it that there are opposing views regarding who the ninja was, in both their origins and how they operated? Why is it that the media and literature portray them as sword-swinging acrobats who perform amazing daredevil feats, when in actuality they were more like secretive cloak-and-dagger envoys than combative martial artists?

Of course, as death defying action heroes that may seem more exciting to some. And the fantasy of being someone with supreme talents and physical skills easily draws the human ego.

As mentioned earlier in this text, much of what occurred back during the ninja heyday centuries ago was not recorded, and to get caught by the opposition with materials during that period could get an individual a death sentence. While there is plenty of records concerning the Samurai and their history documentation is scarce.

Therefore, sellers and promoters of various materials during the Twentieth Century had little to work with, and were forced to fill in the blanks via hearsay, speculation, or possibly their own imaginations.

Commercialism

Plus, let us not discount the huge commercial aspect involved. Due to the public's fascination with these secretive men, and those who love daring tales of swordsmen ones who perform incredible daredevil feats, Ninjutsu has spiraled into a multimillion-dollar business in the U.S., Japan, and even other parts of the globe.

Anything with the Ninja brand seems to draw public attention. The fact that putting the name 'ninja' on a book, comic, cartoon, game, kitchen appliances, flicks, TV show, dojo, or whatever else, can potentially make money.

Have you heard of the Ninja blender, the Ninja motorcycle, and the Ninja television game show that features an obstacle course?

Heresy

Writers such as myself and certain others (see references at end of this book) risk the possibility of getting branded as heretics among their community. By exposing the authenticity of actual ninja mechanisms compared to the fraud that has been thrust upon public, their money-making opportunities feel threatened. Therefore, they have gone as far as banning certain authors from their establishments and are not welcomed in other avenues.

The Big Question

Would you prefer to sit in a theater or in front of a television screen and watch a more factual story about actual ninjas, meaning those who performed "cat and mouse" undercover work, minus all the deadly sword

slinging martial arts action and high-flying stunts? Or, could you care less about fact-based drama stories and want rip-roaring pictures that feature "the more action the better", regardless if they were based on truth or not?

And, what about the children? Ever wonder about how many kids yell 'Trick-or-treat!' on Halloween night while clad as ninjas with their fake plastic swords and rubber nunchuks? Should we spoil their creative fun and tell them the factual truth? Of course not.

That's like telling them about the Tooth Fairy and Santa Claus.

THE SEARCH FOR NINJA TRUTH

Personally, in my opinion I feel most authors and teachers who write about this topic probably have good intentions. Mankind's biggest problem lies in the fact that they cannot travel back in time several hundred years to discover the truth. Therefore, we must rely on the scraps of information left behind during that period.

Did they come from the Iga and Koga regions? That was once the position taken by Stephen Turnball. In a two-page article he wrote "The ninja tradition is an invented tradition", he reversed his position. My hat is off to that author, to whom the author of this book now understands ninja truths and myths much better.

Both he and Antony Cummins, who does similar work and research, deserves credit as well. In my opinion, they are two of the most influential people who aided in the search for ninja truth. Their efforts are much appreciated.

BOOKS OF INTEREST

Here is a list of books which the author has either read or reviewed and thought he would pass them on. **PLEASE NOTE:** I am neither promoting them nor condemning them.

The Grandmaster's Book of Ninja Training, Author-Masaaki Hatsumi.

This incredible book includes a series of very rare interviews with the Grandmaster of Ninja, plus countless rare photos demonstrating the use of the Japanese Naginata. This is a curved one-edged sword mounted on a pole. It is a Japanese weapon that is often seen as a polearm or a spear that could possibly beat the Katana. The content of this relevant and historic volume makes it one of the most interesting and valuable books in regarding the shinobi's past, with a hundred pages of great, inside particulars rarely ever taught or shown outside of old Japan. This book is a must read for anyone interested in the martial arts in general and the ways of the ninja most specifically.

Ninjutsu: History and Tradition, Author-Masaaki Hatsumi

The higher order of ninjutsu should be offered to the world as a guiding influence for all martial artists. The physical and spiritual survival methods eventually immortalized by Japan's Ninja were in fact one of the sources of Japanese martial arts. Without complete and total training in all aspects of the combative arts, today's martial artist cannot hope to progress any further than mere proficiency in the limited set of muscular skills that make up his or her training system.

Personal enlightenment can only come about through total immersion in the martial tradition as a way of living. By experiencing the confrontation of danger, the transcendence of fear, injury or death, and a working knowledge of individual personal skills and limitations, the practitioner of ninjutsu can gain the strength and invincibility that permit enjoyment of the flowers moving in the wind, appreciation of the love of others, and contentment with the presence of peace in society.

The attainment of this enlightenment is characterized by the development of the jihi no kokoro, or benevolent heart. Stronger than love itself, the benevolent heart is capable of encompassing all that constitutes universal justice and all that finds expression in the unfolding of the universal scheme.

Born of the insight attained from repeated exposure to the very brink between life and death, ninpo's benevolent heart is the key to finding harmony and understanding in the realms of the spiritual and natural material worlds. After so many generations of obscurity in the shadowy recesses of yesteryear, their life philosophy is now once again emerging, because once again, it is the time in human destiny in which ninpo is needed. May peace prevail so that mankind may continue to grow and evolve into the next great plateau.

The Complete Ninja: The Secret World Revealed, Author-Masaaki Hatsumi

These fighters were the true embodiment of budo, the warrior spirit. Rather than using the methodology of assassination to protect themselves, they relied on their senses, and on an acute awareness of their natural surroundings, in fact, they avoided unnecessary conflict, using weapons such as knives and swords only as a last resort. These are the true techniques of ninjutsu, and the art in which the ninja unrelentingly trained.

Masaaki Hatsumi, the world's most renowned ninja grandmaster and top budo master, creates a companion volume to his best-selling The Way of the Ninja. Like the earlier work, The Complete Ninja features hundreds of historical illustrations, documents, and photos (including many of the author demonstrating them) to explore the essence and wisdom of ninjutsu and reveal its hidden truths.

The Complete Ninja will help readers sharpen their perceptions and deepen their understanding of two core principles: that ninjutsu is the very backbone of the martial arts, and that it clarifies their essential spiritual significance. Since budo transcends any one particular martial tradition, all practitioners, whether they study judo, aikido, karate, kendo, kenjutsu, jujutsu, or other combative sports, will find the book fascinating and enlightening.

The Ninja and Their Secret Fighting Art, Author-Stephen K. Hayes

Look past the legends and lore and learn about the REAL ninjas of feudal Japan with this entertaining, illustrated ninjutsu guide.

Ninjutsu, the least understood of the Japanese martial arts, is an ancient fighting style emphasizing natural movement, responsiveness to adversaries, and absolute practicality. In feudal Japan, these guerrillas were feared for their skill in infiltration and, particularly murder. Masters of weaponry, stealth, and martial operations, ninja were credited with supernatural powers because of the near-invincibility of their unique and deadly art.

In The Ninja and their Secret Fighting Art, Black Belt Hall of Fame member, Stephen K. Hayes, reveals the secrets that lead to the perception of the ninja as individuals of almost sorcerous skill, such as the art of invisibility, special tools and weapons, and psychological training enabling them to gain advantage in any situation.

Ninjutsu: The Art of the Invisible Warrior, Author-Stephen K. Hayes

This book offers self-defense enthusiasts a comprehensive guide to the mysterious and ancient art of the ninja, written by one of the Western world's foremost authority, Stephen Hayes. Profusely illustrated with more than 580 action photographs and diagrams, this book clearly shows the correct body positions and style for mastering the ninja method.

Exercises such as hitting the ground and rebounding safely, shifting, and evading strikes and weapon hits, and applying natural body weapons and handheld tools for combat are covered in detail. The book's physical conditioning program includes training exercises for increasing flexibility and building muscle strength, followed by footwork drills, reaction drills, counter actions, and combat skills.

Of equal importance to this ancient art is the spiritual training. Hayes provides all movement and meditation pondering, essential to their combat style.

Ninja Vol.1: Spirit of the Shadow Warrior, Author-Stephen K. Hayes

Ninja Spirit of the Shadow Warrior is the first installment in Hayes' quest to uncover the secrets of the Ninjas. In this book Hayes introduces his readers to Ninjutsu's, basic postures, fighting maneuvers and weapons. The author also teaches meditation exercises to strengthen consciousness and decrease reaction time. Discover where the Shinobi came from, what they did, how they survived, and where they are now. An overall awesome read.

Ninja Vol.2: the Warriors Way of Enlightenment, Author-Stephen K. Hayes

Ninja Volume II the Warrior Ways, introduces combat principles, such as dealing with and avoiding danger, ground rolls and rebounds, training for modern altercations, and the intense generating hand symbols of kuji-in. In Volume II, the author has added more advanced tools and concepts to a more modern training regimen. This book continues where Volume I left off and is ideal for anyone interested in the Ninjutsu arts.

Ninjitsu The Art of Invisibility, Author-Donn F. Draegar

"Ninjutsu", the ancient and secret Japanese art of espionage and assassination, has long fascinated the Western world. Ninja masters were adept in the martial arts and prowess of cunning and concealment. Stripping away the myth and mystery, Donn Draeger reveals the secrets that have earned the ninja a reputation as some of the most feared agents ever.

Ninja Weapons: Chain and Shuriken, Author- Charles V. Gruzanski

This informative martial arts book, Ninja Weapons introduces the exciting and deadly secrets of ninjutsu—the chain and the shuriken.

The Masaki school of chain fighting was developed in the feudal society of the early eighteenth century by a swordsman-sentry in Edo (Tokyo) Castle. Feeling that the shedding of blood in such a hallowed place would be disgraceful, he devised the combat use of the weighted chain. Even the name he gave to the art proves the trust he placed in its effectiveness – manrikigusari (chain with the power of ten thousand).

The equally devastating art of shuriken, the throwing of metal stars and spikes, evolved shortly after manrikigusari. The easily concealed shuriken soon became known as an extremely effective weapon for both shinobi and samurai individuals. Included are "The Samurai Creed," various systems, the history of the arts and over a hundred black and white photos and illustrations.

The Illustrated Ninja Handbook: Hidden Techniques of Ninjutsu, Author-Remigiusz Borda

Learn to master the ninjutsu ways and the Budo warrior ethos with this informative and entertaining martial arts guide.

Welcome to the secret world of the ninja master! Here is a fundamental manual to the esoteric knowledge and teachings of the ancient Japanese shinobi. It provides ninjutsu devotees with the first detailed understanding of this shadowy and mysterious martial art form.

It contains step-by-step instructions that allow you to master the forty most devastating ninja fighting styles. Created with the blessing of legendary ninjutsu master Soke Masaaki Hatsumi, who taught for many generations in the Bujinkan School he is recognized by many to be the leading ninjutsu school in the world.

The Bujinkan Dojo encompasses nine separate ryu-ha or martial arts schools that are based in Japan and headed by Hatsumi. Bujinkan ninjas use both armed and unarmed fighting movements, with weapons such as swords, bamboo shinai, and staffs. They also learn to defend themselves unarmed against weapons attacks. Author Remigiusz Borda studied and taught Bujinkan ninjutsu for many decades, and in this book presents the unique system created by Masaaki Hatsumi—the 34th Grandmaster and head of the Togakure-ryu Ninjutsu lineage.

The Illustrated Ninja Handbook is based on hundreds of years of actual ninja combat experience and contains the traditional knowledge of the legendary Shinobi warriors who were instrumental in helping found the Tokugawa Shogunate.

Ninja Skills: the Authentic Ninja Training Manual, Author-Antony Cummins

One of the world's only illustrated guides to the real ninja teachings of historic Japan with original methods presented in a highly accessible 'how-to' format.

The shadowy figure of the expert commando, secret agent, maverick who operates outside social norms— continues to exert fascination in the West, yet much of what is presented as ninja fact today is distorted or wrong.

Drawing on the scrolls created by actual Japanese ninjas (or shinobi, as they were then known), this book offers the real teachings in one hundred fifty easy-to-follow, illustrated lessons designed to draw contemporary students of ninja straight into the world of these skilled spy-commandos.

The truth about the ninja is so much more complex and intriguing than the Hollywood clichés we know today. We may think, for example, of them as being always garbed in black and fighting with 'throwing stars' but in fact, they had clothes in different colors to serve under cover for different times of day, and their arsenal of weaponry could include anything from various poisons, poison gas, pepper spray and fire-creating tools to swords, spears, and knives (but no throwing stars).

The one hundred fifty lessons in this book cover all the basics of war craft, including clever ideas for infiltrating an enemy compound (from wearing 'silent sandals' to faking passes and passwords), tactics for hiding and retreat (in the racoon dog retreat, one would crouch low and halt, allowing the pursuer to collide with him at speed, whereupon he could kill his enemy), along with ways of crossing marshes and water (for example, with special shoes made of boards, or using a foldaway floating seat). The description is made all the more vivid by step-by-step photographs of the fighting action diagrams outlining military tactics and beautiful samples of Japanese calligraphy.

MOVIES

This section will fade in and close with a couple of ninja films. Be warned that while these movies were popular and highly entertaining none of them portray ninjas as they actually were. Still, sit back, relax, and get the popcorn ready if you plan on watching any of these.

American Ninja is a 1985 American martial arts action feature produced by Menahem Golan and Yoram Globus's Cannon Films. Directed by Sam Firstenberg, who specialized in this genre in the 1980s, it stars Michael Dudikoff in the title role and is the first installment in the American Ninja franchise, followed by American Ninja 2: The Confrontation (1987). It had a mixed reception, but it was a financial success, and since then, it has been considered a cult movie.

Ninja Assassin

A 2009 neo-noir martial arts film directed by James McTeigue. The story was written by Matthew Sand, with a screenplay by J. Michael Straczynski. It stars South Korean pop musician Rain as a disillusioned assassin looking for retribution against his former mentor, played by ninja silver screen legend Sho Kosugi. It explores political corruption, child endangerment and the impact of violence. The Wachowskis, Joel Silver, and Grant Hill produced it for Legendary Pictures, Dark Castle Entertainment and Silver Pictures. It was distributed by Warner Bros. Pictures.

Ninja is a 2009 American martial arts movie directed by Isaac Florentine and starring Scott Adkins,

Tsuyoshi Ihara and Mika Hijii. Its plot revolves around an American martial artist named Casey Bowman, who is asked by his sensei to travel to New York City and protect the Yoroi Bitsu, an armored chest that contains the weapons of the last Kōga ninja.

Shadow of a Tear is a sequel to the movie.

Ninja Scroll

A 1993 Japanese animated jidaigeki-chanbara film written and directed by Yoshiaki Kawajiri, starring the voices of Kōichi Yamadera, Emi Shinohara, Takeshi Aono, Daisuke Gōri, Toshihiko Seki and Shūichirō Moriyama. It was a co-production between JVC, Toho and Movic, with Madhouse serving as the animation studio. It was theatrically released in Japan on June 5, 1993, and received an English-dubbed release produced by Metro-Goldwyn-Mayer and released in Western countries through Manga Entertainment in 1995.

Praised for its animation and action scenes, Ninja Scroll is regarded by many as one of the most influential anime movies ever made. Alongside Akira and Ghost in the Shell, it was responsible for increasing the popularity of adult-oriented anime outside of Japan.

It has been cited by The Wachowskis as an influence on the Matrix franchise, and resulted in Kawajiri later contributing to two segments of the anthology film The Animatrix.

A televised stand-alone sequel, Ninja Scroll: The Series, was aired in Japan in 2003.

Raven (American TV series)

Raven is an American martial arts drama series that first aired on CBS from June 19, 1992 to April 30, 1993.

Jonathon Raven is a ninja-trained former Special Forces agent, retired in Hawaii to search for his long-lost son. Avoiding assassins sent to kill him by his former associates in the Black Dragon's, he uses his skills to help those in need. He is assisted by his former military buddy turned eccentric private investigator, Herman Jablonski.

Shinobi No Mono Collection

'Ninja, Band of Assassins' ('Shinobi no Mono', A.K.A 'Tales of The Ninja' or 'The Ninja') is a series of eight jidaigeki (Japanese historical dramas which were released in Japan over a four-year period from 1962 to 1966 by Daiei

Pictures. The plot of the first few films focuses on a ninja named Ishikawa Goemon and his struggle to survive during Japan's warring states period. It stars Ichikawa Raizo (of Nemuri Kyoshiro / Sleepy Eyes of Death fame) who plays Ishikawa Goemon as well as several other characters throughout the series, such as Kirigakure Saizo, Hattori Hanzo & Fuma Kotaro. Wakayama Tomisaburo (of Kozure Ookami / Lone Wolf and Cub fame) also appears in the first four features.

Sho Kosugi

Sho Kosugi born Shōichi Kosugi on June 17, 1948, is a Japanese actor with extensive training in Shindō jinen-ryū Karate, Kendo, Judo, Iaido, Kobudo, Aikido and Ninjutsu. A former All Japan Karate Champion, he gained popularity as an actor during the 1980s, often playing ninjas. He starred in a trilogy of martial arts ninja movies produced by Cannon Films (Enter the Ninja, Revenge of the Ninja, and Ninja III: The Domination), before starring in the primetime television series The Master. His work helped establish ninjas in popular culture, leading to a "ninja boom" or "ninjamania" during the early-to-mid-1980s.

Life and career

At the age of 19, Kosugi left Japan to study and reside in Los Angeles where he earned a bachelor's degree in Economics at CSULA. At the same time, he consistently improved his martial arts skills while learning a wide variety of styles, such as Chinese Xing Yi Quan, Korean taekwondo and Japanese Shitō-ryū and Shotokan-ryū karate.

He is the father of Kane Kosugi and Shane Kosugi, who are both actors and martial artists, and Ayeesha Kosugi, a former senior member of the women's golf team at the University of Las Vegas. After taking a hiatus from the silver screen, he started a taiko group in California. In Japan, he also ran an internationally oriented bunch of martial arts acting schools known as the Sho Kosugi Institute. He currently resides in Los Angeles. Productions in which Kosugi's sons perform alongside their father include Revenge of the Ninja,

Pray for Death, Black Eagle, and Journey of Honor (A.K.A. Kabuto, Shogun Mayeda and Shogun Warrior).

In 2009, Sho made a comeback to movies playing the lead villain of Ozunu in the action thriller Ninja Assassin opposite K-pop star and actor Rain.

Sho Kosugi Films

1981 Enter the Ninja

1983 Revenge of the Ninja Cho Osaki

1984 Ninja III: The Domination

1985 9 Deaths of the Ninja Pray for Death

1987 Rage of Honor Black Eagle

1989 Blind Fury

The Hunted

The Hunted is a 1995 American and Japanese martial-arts thriller written and directed by J. F. Lawton in his mainstream directorial debut, and starring Christopher Lambert, John Lone, Joan Chen, Yoshio Harada and Yoko Shimada. Lambert plays Paul Racine, an American businessman who by accident earns the wrath of shinobi folks led by Lone's character, Kinjo.

It was shot in Nagoya, Japan, and Vancouver, British Columbia, Canada on a $25 million budget, and premiered in February 1995, taking in $6.6 million in U.S. box office. Most critic reviews found the plot clichéd and the acting unconvincing, while some praised Harada's performance as samurai Ijuro Takeda, Racine's protector and Kinjo's sworn enemy. The critically well-received soundtrack featured music by the Japanese taiko troupe Kodō, which pervades the film.

The Master

The Master is an American action-adventure television series which aired on NBC, from January to August 1984. Created by Michael Sloan, the series focuses on the adventures of John Peter McAllister (Lee Van Cleef), an aging ninja master, and his young pupil, Max Keller (Timothy Van Patten). Most episodes focus on the mismatched pair driving around in a custom van, helping people in need along the way, similar to the contemporary NBC television series, The A-Team. The Master lasted 13 episodes before it was canceled.

The Octagon

The Octagon is a 1980 American action martial arts picture starring Chuck Norris, Karen Carlson, and Lee Van Cleef. It was directed by Eric Karson and written by Paul Aaron and Leigh Chapman. This one involves a martial artist (Norris) who must stop a gang of terrorists trained in the ninja style by his half-brother (Tadashi Yamashita).

The Samurai (TV series)

The Samurai is a Japanese fiction television series made by Senkosha Productions during the early 1960s. Its original Japanese title was Onmitsu Kenshi ("Spy Swordsman"). The series premiered in 1962 on TBS and ran continuously until 1965 for ten self-contained story arcs (seasons), usually of 13 episodes each. Also created were two black-and-white features by Toei Company, made in 1964 by the same crew which created the TV series, and a stage show.

The Samurai proved to be highly successful despite its very limited budget. It was the first Japanese TV program ever screened in Australia, where it premiered in 1964 and built up a remarkably large fan-base among the local young audience at the time, rapidly becoming a cult favorite. Despite its massive popularity in Australia as well as success in Japan, New Zealand and the Philippines, the series was not widely screened elsewhere and its fame remains largely restricted to those countries.

The series portrayed the adventures of a roving samurai detective, Akikusa Shintarō (played by Koichi Ose), whose real identity is Matsudaira Nobuchiyo - the older half-brother of Tokugawa Ienari, the 11th Tokugawa shogun, who is still a minor. Because he is the son of a concubine, Nobuchiyo has no claim to authority, so he assumes the guise of a wandering swordsman named Shintarō to seek out and eliminate plots by rival feudal lords and thus protect his younger brother.

Initially it was planned to make only four distinct stories, with a different hero in each, however Shintaro was received so well that he remained for the rest of the series in which, acting on secret orders from the rōjū (high councillor) Lord Matsudaira Sadanobu, he gathers material mostly in the various fiefdoms of the central Honshū and battles rival mercenaries and spies, often aided by his faithful assistant Tombei the Mist (Kiri no Tonbei) (played by Fuyukichi Maki).

VARIOUS TITLES:

Spy Swordsman (Onmitsu Kenshi)

Koga Ninjas (Ninpō Kōgashū)

Iga Ninjas (Ninpō Iga Jūnin)

Black Ninja (Ninpō Yami Hōshi)

Fuma Ninja (Ninpō Fūma Ichizoku)

Fuma Ninja Continued (Zoku Ninpō Fūma Ichizoku)

Ninja Terror (Ninpō Negoru-Shū)

Phantom Ninja (Ninpō Mabaroshi-Shū)

Puppet Ninja (Kugotsu Ninpōchō)

Contest of Death (Ayakashi Ninpōchō)

*FAMED NINJAS WHO ACTUALLY EXISTED

Hattori Hanzō

Born 1542. Died November 14, 1597 (age 55) Nicknamed "Demon Hanzō", was a famous ninja of the Sengoku era, who served the Tokugawa clan, credited with saving the life of Tokugawa Ieyasu and then helping him to become the ruler of united Japan. He is often a subject of varied portrayal in modern popular culture. Hanzō was known as an expert tactician and a master of sword fighting.

He would later earn the nickname "Demon Hanzō" because of the fearless tactics he displayed in his operations. Though Hanzō was born in Mikawa Province (now Iga-chō, Okazaki, Aichi), he often returned to Iga Province, home of the Hattori's at the age of 16, his first battle was a night time attack during the siege of Udo Castle. At the time, he commanded seventy Iga ninja.

Hanzo had a great contribution to Tokugawa Ieyasu's rise to prominence helping the future Shogun bring down the Imagawa's. After Imagawa Ujizane had held Ieyasu's wife and son as hostages in 1561, Hanzo made a successful hostage rescue of Tokugawa's family at Kaminogo castle in 1562 and went on to lay siege to Kakegawa castle in 1569 against the Imagawa's

He served with distinction at the battles of Anegawa in 1570 and Mikatagahara in 1572. According to the Kansei Chōshū Shokafu, a genealogy of major samurai completed in 1812 by the Tokugawa shogunate, Hattori Hanzō rendered meritorious service during the Battle of Mikatagahara and became commander of an Iga unit consisting of one hundred fifty men. He captured a Takeda agent named Chikuan, and when Takeda's troops invaded Totomi, Hanzō counterattacked with only thirty men at the Tenryū River.

His most valuable contribution came in 1582 following Oda Nobunaga's death, when he led the future shōgun Tokugawa Ieyasu to safety in Mikawa Province across Iga territory with the help of remnants of the local Iga-ryū ji-samurai family as well as Kōga-ryū the neighboring local samurai tribes in the nearby

Koka region. Hanzo was principal in serving as Ieyasu's guide and commanded 300 shinobi guards to ensure his lord's safe passage to Mikawa.

In 1584, Hattori Hanzo continued to serve his lord at Battle of Komaki and Nagakute with a hundred warriors under his command.

In 1590, Hattori Hanzo served during the Odawara campaign and was awarded 8,000 kokus. By the time Ieyasu entered Kantō, he was awarded an additional 8,000 koku and had 30 yoriki and 200 public officials for his services. Ieyasu was said to have also begun to employ more Iga shinobi with Hanzō as their leader.

While he died at the age of 55 in 1597, there are two theories about his death. One asserts that he was assassinated by a rival Samurai, the pirate Fūma Kotarō. After Hanzo tracked him down to the Inland Sea, Kotarō lured him and his men into a small channel and used oil to set the channel on fire. The second theory is that Hanzo became a monk in Edo where he lived out the rest of his days until he died of illness.

Historical sources say he lived the last several years of his life as a monk under the name "Sainen" and built the temple Sainenji, which was named after him, mainly built to commemorate Tokugawa Ieyasu's elder son, Tokugawa Nobuyasu.

After Nobuyasu was accused of treason and conspiracy by Oda Nobunaga was then ordered to commit seppuku by his father, Ieyasu. Hanzo was called in to act as the official second to end Nobuyasu's suffering, but he refused to take the sword with the blood of his own lord. Ieyasu valued his loyalty after hearing of Hanzo's ordeal and said, "Even a demon can shed tears."

Legacy

Edo Castle's Hanzōmon gate during the Meiji period (1868–1912). Hanzo's reputation as a samurai leader who commanded a two hundred-men strong unit of Iga warriors has grown to legendary proportions. Tales of Hattori's exploits often attributed various extraordinary abilities, such as teleportation, psychokinesis, and precognition.

After his death on 4 November 1596, Hattori Hanzō was succeeded by his son, whose name was also Masanari (third Hanzō), though written with different kanji (instead of). He was given the title of Iwami no Kami and his Iga men would act as guards of Edo Castle, the headquarters of the government of united Japan. Hanzō is actually a name passed down through the leaders of the Hattori relatives meaning his father was also called Hanzō and so was his successor. Indeed, there are five people known as Hattori Hanzō throughout time.

The Tokyo Imperial Palace Hanzōmon Gate

To this day, artifacts of Hanzō's legacy remain. Tokyo Imperial Palace (formerly the shōgun's palace) still has a gate called Hanzō's Gate (Hanzōmon), and the Hanzōmon subway line which runs from Hanzōmon Station in central Tokyo to the southwestern suburbs is named after the gate, where his house was once located. The neighborhood outside Hanzō's Gate is known as Wakaba, but before 1943 was named Iga-chō ("Iga Town"). Hanzō's remains now rest in the Sainen-ji temple cemetery in Yotsuya, Tokyo. The temple also holds his favorite spear and his ceremonial battle helmet. The spear, originally 14 feet (4.3 m) long and given to him by Ieyasu, was donated to the temple by Hanzō as a votive offering, but was damaged during the bombing of Tokyo in 1945.

Momochi Sandayu

Momochi Sandayu (approx. 1525-1585) is one of the most legendary ninjas in the history of feudal Japan, a descendant of the Otomo family, from the Iga region, an area that was controlled by three famous ninja groups: the Hattori's, the Fujibayashi's and the Momochi families.

Momochi Sandayu became Sôke of several schools, including Hakuun Ryu Ninpo, Gyokko Ryu Koshijutsu, Koto Ryu Koppojutsu and Momochi Ryu. Very active in the Tembun era (1542-1555), he served the Sanada's in this turbulent Japanese era and was the master of several other famous ninja such as Hanzo Hattori and Ishikawa Goemon.

In order to hinder his capture and hide his identity, it is said that Sandayu came to have three different homes and three families, without any of them knowing about the existence of the other two. Their homes were Ryugu Castle, Hojiro Castle and Yamato Castle. In each castle he had a different personality as well as all the necessary resources to escape in case of danger.

In November of 1581 the invasion of the province of Iga by the troops of the Shogun Oda Nobunaga took place to end the power of the shinobi of the area, and there the famous battle called "Tensho Iga No Ran" was played in the which most of the ninja of the different clans were massacred and the survivors spread throughout the country.

The chronicles say that Momochi Sandayu fought fiercely in battle and managed to flee with one of his men hiding in the east of the country and settling under the guise of a farmer in the province of Kii until he learned the news of Nobunaga's murder, at the hands of one of his own generals, on June 10, 1582.

One of the versions says that Momochi Sandayu then returned to Iga and tried to unite the Momochi and Hattori clans, but that attempt failed and there were many internal fights between the two gangs. Finally, leaders, Momochi Sandayu and Hattori Hanzo dueled, Momochi Sandayu died at the hands of his former student.

Other versions of the story suggest that he disappeared and was never heard from again after his escape and hiding in the province of Kii.

His grave was discovered in the 1960's near one of their homes, south of Iga-Ueno. Kuden of Momochi Sandayu.

Fūma Kotarō was the name adopted by the leader of the ninja Fūma clan during the Sengoku era of feudal Japan. He was retainer of Later Hōjō clan. According to some records, his name was initially Kazama Kotarō.

The fūma clan and fūma kotarō were based in Kanagawa Prefecture, specializing in horseback guerrilla warfare and naval reconnaissance. According to some sources, they had roots in the tenth century when they served Taira no Masakado in his revolt against the Kyoto government. The use of the name started with the first leader (jonin): originally surnamed (Fūma), with a different kanji. Each subsequent leader of the school adopted the same name as its founder, making it difficult to identify them individually. This school was in the service of the Hōjō clan of Odawara.

Fūma Kotarō was the fifth and the best known of the Fūma leaders. Born in Sagami Province (modern Kanagawa Prefecture) on an unknown date, he became notorious as the leader of a band of 200 Rappa "battle disrupters", divided into four categories: brigands, pirates, burglars, and thieves. Kotarō served under Hōjō Ujimasa and Hōjō Ujinao. His biggest achievement came in 1580 at Battle of Omosu, when the Fūma ninja covertly infiltrated and attacked a camp of the Takeda tribe forces under Takeda Katsuyori at night, succeeding in causing severe chaos in the camp, which resulted in massive casualties among the disoriented enemies as they attacked each other. Later In 1590, at Siege of Odawara, when Toyotomi Hideyoshi laid a blockage to Odawara Castle, which eventually fell, and the Hōjō line was forced to surrender.

When the Tokugawa shogunate came to sovereignty, the remnants of Fūma-ryū were reduced to a band of brigands operating in and around Edo. A popular but fictional story says that in 1596, Kotarō was responsible for the death of Hattori Hanzō, a famous ninja in the service of Tokugawa Ieyasu, who had tracked him down in the Inland Sea, but Kotarō has succeeded in luring him into a small channel, where a tide trapped the Tokugawa gunboats and his men then set fire to the channel with oil.

Kotarō was eventually caught by the Tokugawa shogunate's special law-enforcement force, guided by his rival and a former Takeda shinobi Kōsaka Jinnai, and executed through beheading by an order of Ieyasu in 1603.

Katō Danzō (1503 – 1569) was a famed 16th century ninja master during the Sengoku period Japan who was also known as flying Katō (Tobi Katō).

There are many versions of his story and many mysteries surround him. According to the legend he practiced sorcery, performing amazing feats such as swallowing a bull in front of the crowd of over twenty people; his alias comes from his alleged capacity to fly. Some researchers believe his reported magical arts were illusion as a type of group hypnosis. However, this belief has never been proven to be the case and therefore is only considered to be a possibility. His date of birth and death are unknown.

According to early records, the daimyō Uesugi Kenshin had heard of Danzō's reputation, which had led for him to invite Danzō to his prime castle. Kenshin decided to test Danzō's abilities by challenging him to sneak into a certain castle and to retrieve a prized naginata (a sword in another version of this story) from one of his retainers, Naoe Kanetsugu.

Danzō infiltrated Kanetsugu's heavily guarded castle and not only succeeding in stealing the naginata, but also captured a young servant girl. Kenshin then realized that Danzō would be a very useful ally and took him into his service. However, Kanetsugu plotted to kill Danzō (according to another version it was Kenshin himself who ordered his death, perceiving him to be too skillful and thus dangerous), forcing him to try to defect to Takeda Shingen, Kenshin's rival.

Suspecting Danzō to be a double agent, Shingen however ordered him to be killed. Danzō was captured by Takeda's men and executed through decapitation. (Takeda Shingen was daimyo of Kai Province during the Sengoku period of Japan. Known as the "Tiger of Kai".)

Jinichi Kawakami

Born in 1949, head of Banke Shinobinoden, is the last sōke and only heir to authentic ninjutsu. He says he is the 21st head of the Koga Ban family (Iga and Koga Ninjutsu), a mercenary, and the honorary director of the Iga-ryu Ninja Museum. In 2011, he was specially appointed a professor at Mie University to research ninjutsu at the university's research cooperation center.

Kawakami boasts no ninja bloodline of his own, but says he learned his art as a boy from a man named Masado (Masazo) Ishida, a medicine peddler claiming to be one of the last remaining ninjutsu practitioners alive. According to Japan Times, "Kawakami has something most other shinobi claimants do not — an earnest combination of humility and scholarship. Not to mention some highly polished martial arts skills of his own." He is also a former trained engineer.

His top student, Yasushi Kiyomoto, is the only one teaching from the Banke Shinobinoden group. Kiyomoto operates a dojo in Sagamihara-shi, Kanagawa Prefecture, but he no longer takes on new students.

In 2012, Kawakami decided that he will not appoint anyone to take over as the next ninja grandmaster. He told BBC News: "In the age of civil wars or during the Edo period, ninjas' know-how to spy and kill, or mix medicine may have been useful. But we now have guns, the internet and much better medicines, so the art of ninjutsu has no place in the modern age."

Jinichi Kawakami and his student Yasushi Kiyomoto were first introduced to the anglophone world in the book, A Story of Life, Fate, and Finding the Lost Art of Koga Ninjutsu in Japan first published in 2008.

THE QUIZ

How well do you know ninjas?

For fun you may wish to take this quiz to find out.

Answers are provided at the end of this section.

QUESTIONS:

(1) Did ninjas wear black uniforms?

(2) Did they carry Samurai Katana swords?

(3) Were ninjas assassins?

(4) Were they exceptional martial artists?

(5) Did ninjas use throwing stars?

(6) Did they use firearms?

(7) Did they use nunchakus?

(8) Did ninja train from childhood?

(9) Are ninja operating today?

(10) Were they capable of mystical and magical feats?

(11) What is a Female Ninja called?

(12) What is a Dojo?

(13) Kusarigama is what kind of a weapon?

(14) How would you use a Yumi and a Ya?

(15) The act of suicide is known as?

(16) Did Ninjas originate espionage?

(17) Which martial arts did they practice?

(18) How did they climb trees?

(19) Could they fly utilizing large kites?

(20) Could outsiders join a Ninja clan?

ANSWERS

(1) Did ninjas wear black uniforms? A popular argument is that ninja did not wear black but rather they wore blue. For Further Clarification See Chapter Titled: **UNIFORMS**

(2) Did they carry Samurai katana swords? Only actual Samurai were privileged to those. It was illegal for anyone to own or carry a real Samurai sword unless you were an actual Samurai. For Further Clarification See Chapter Titled: **SWORDS**

(3) Were Ninjas Assassins? Espionage was the chief role of the ninja. As cloak and dagger agents they spent more time in the investigative business rather than in the assassination trade. For Further Clarification See Chapter Titled: **ASSASSINS**

(4) Were they exceptional martial artists? Since the primary function of the ninja was the act of deception, hand-to-hand combat would have been a secondary skill. For Further Clarification See Chapter Titled: **MARTIAL ARTS**

(5) Did Ninjas use throwing stars? No. Actually they used throwing spikes. Sharp-pointed throwing stars were a weapon used in various Samurai schools and only became linked to ninjas through movies, comic books, and animation. For Further Clarification See Chapter Titled: **WEAPONRY**

(6) Did they use firearms? The introduction of guns from the Western world to Japan was in 1543. Ninja would likely use anything to their advantage, including firearms, when they could obtain them. For Further Clarification See Chapter Titled: **GUNPOWDER**

(7) Did they use nunchakus? The Wood-handled nunchakus made famous by silver screen legend Bruce Lee weren't known to be battlefield weapons they were considered ineffective against long armament such as swords and spears. For Further Clarification See Chapter Titled: **WEAPONRY**

(8) Did Ninjas train from childhood? Running, jumping, and climbing events were encouraged by parents and concealed as games. For Further Clarification See Chapter Titled: **TRAINING**

(9) Are Ninja operating today? If you want to become a real ninja, you might be better off joining the military or the CIA rather than studying at an indoor martial arts dojo. For Further Clarification See Chapter Titled: **NINJAS TODAY**

(10) Were they capable of mystical and magical feats? Incredible feats such as walking on water, walking thru walls, shape shifting, and even disappearing into thin air are all part of the legend. For Further Clarification See Chapter Titled: **MAGIC**

(11) What is a Female Ninja called? Kunoichi. For Further Clarification See Chapter Titled: **LABELS**

(12) What is a Dojo? A school for training in various arts of self-defense. For Further Clarification See Chapter Titled: **SCHOOLS**

(13) Kusarigama is what kind of a weapon? A metal chain (kusari) or sickle with a heavy iron weight attached. For Further Clarification See Chapter Titled: **WEAPONRY**

(14) How would you use a Yumi and a Ya? As a bow & an arrow. For Further Clarification See Chapter Titled: **ARMAMENTS**

(15) The act of suicide is known as? Hara Kiri or seppuku. For Further Clarification See Chapter Titled: **CAPTURE**

(16) Did Ninjas originate espionage? No. Espionage had been practiced by many cultures since the beginning of written history. For Further Clarification See Book Titled: **Ninjitsu the Art of Invisibility.**

(17) Which martial arts did they practice? The ninja excelled in all the martial arts of their day, such as kendo, kyudo and naginata-do. For Further Clarification See Chapter Titled: **MARTIAL ARTS**

(18) How did they climb trees? With shuko hand claws and foot spikes. For Further Clarification See Chapter Titled: **TOOLS**

(19) Could they fly utilizing large kites? No. Kites were used for transporting supplies, sending messages, or dropping bombs. For Further Clarification See Chapter Titled: **MAGIC**

(20) Could outsiders join a Ninja clan? Shinobi were born into the profession, where traditions were kept in, and passed down through the family. For Further Clarification See Chapter Titled: **CLANS**

**NINJA: An Encapsulation of Ninja Lore and History.

A ninja or shinobi (defined as "to sneak") was a covert surrogate or mercenary in feudal Japan. Their functions included cunning, sabotage, infiltration, killing and guerrilla warfare. The shinobi proper, a specially trained batch of spies, appeared in the 15th century during the Sengoku period, but ancestors may have existed as far back as the 14th century, and possibly in the 12th century (Heian or early Kamakura era).

A number of shinobi manuals, often based on Chinese military philosophy, were written in the 17th and 18th centuries, most notably the Bansenshukai (1676).

By the time of the Meiji Restoration (1868), the tradition of the shinobi had become a topic of popular imagination and mystery in Japan. They figured prominently in folklore, where they were associated with legendary potential such as invisibility, walking on water and control over the natural elements. As a consequence, their perception in popular culture is often based more on such legend and myths than on the historic accuracy.

Word Origin

The word "ninja" in kanji script

Ninja is an on'yomi (Early Middle Chinese–influenced) reading of the two kanji. (Chinese letters). In the native kun'yomi kanji reading, it is pronounced shinobi, a shortened form of the transcription shinobi-no-mono. The word shinobi appears in the written record as far back as the late 8th century in poems in the Man'yoshu. The underlying connotation means "to steal away; to hide" and "to forbear", hence its association with stealth and invisibility. Mono means "a person".

The word ninja was not in common use, and a variety of regional colloquialisms or vocabularies evolved to describe what would later be dubbed ninja. Some other examples include monomi ("one who sees"), nokizaru ("macaque on the roof"), rappa ("ruffian"), kusa ("grass") and Iga-mono ("one from Iga"). In historical documents, shinobi is almost always used.

In the West, the word ninja became more prevalent than shinobi in the post-World War II culture, possibly because it was easier for Westerners to say. In English, the plural can be either unchanged as ninja, reflecting the Japanese language's lack of grammatical number, or the regular English plural ninjas.

Chronicle

Despite many popular folktale, factual accounts of the ninja are scarce. Stephen Turnbull asserts that they were mostly recruited from the lower class, and therefore little literary interest was taken in them. Instead, war epics such as the Tale of Hogen (Hogen Monogatari) and the Tale of the Heike (Heike Monogatari) focus mainly on the aristocratic samurai, whose deeds were apparently more appealing to the audience.

Historian Kiyoshi Watatani states that they were trained to be particularly secretive about their actions and existence: So-called ninjutsu techniques, in short are the skills of shinobi-no-jutsu and shinobijutsu, which have the aims of ensuring that one's opponent does not know of one's existence, and for which there was special training.

The title ninja has sometimes been attributed retrospectively to the semi-legendary 4th-century prince Yamato Takeru. In the Kojiki, the young Yamato Takeru masked himself as a charming maiden, and murdered two chiefs of the Kumaso people.

However, these records take place at a very early stage of Japanese history, and they are unlikely to be connected to the shinobi of later accounts.

The first recorded use of intelligence collecting was under the employment of Prince Shotoku in the 6th century. Such tactics were considered unsavory even in early times, when, according to the 10th century Shomonki, the boy operative Koharumaru was killed for spying against the insurgent Taira no Masakado. Later, the 14th century war chronicle Taiheiki contained many references to shinobi, and credited the destruction of a castle by fire to an unnamed but "highly skilled shinobi".

Earliest Narrative

It was not until the 15th century that spies were specially trained for their purpose. It was around this time that the word shinobi appeared to define and clearly identify ninja as a secretive band of agents. Evidence for this can be seen in historical reports, which began to refer to these sly soldiers as shinobi during the Sengoku period. Later manuals regarding clandestine activities are often grounded in Chinese military strategy, quoting works such as The Art of War (Sunzi Bingfa) by Sun Tzu.

These antagonists emerged in the 15th century, where they were recruited as spies, raiders, arsonists and even terrorists. Amongst the samurai, a sense of ritual and decorum was observed, where one was expected to fight or duel openly. Combined with the unrest of the Sengoku era, these factors created a demand for men willing to commit deeds considered disreputable for conventional warriors.

By the Sengoku period, the shinobi had several roles, including spy (kancho), scout (teisatsu), surprise attacker (kishu), and agitator (konran). The families were organized into larger guilds, each with their own territories. A system of rank existed. A jonin ("upper man") was the highest rank, representing the group and hiring out operatives. This is followed by the chunin ("middle man"), assistants to the jonin. At the bottom was the genin ("lower man"), field agents drawn from the lower class and assigned to carry out actual missions.

Early papers regarding their origins in these mountainous regions are considered generally correct. The chronicle Go Kagami Furoku writes, "There was a retainer of the family of Kawai Aki-no-kami of Iga, of pre-eminent skill in shinobi, and consequently for generations the name of people from Iga became established. Another tradition grew in Koga."

Likewise, a supplement to the Nochi Kagami, a record of the Ashikaga shogunate, confirms the same Iga origin: Inside the camp at Magari of the Shogun [Ashikaga] Yoshihisa there were shinobi whose names were famous throughout the land. When Yoshihisa attacked Rokkaku Takayori, the faction of Kawai Aki-no-kami of Iga, who served him at Magari, earned considerable merit as shinobi in front of the great army of the Shogun. Since then, successive generations of Iga men have been admired. This is the origin of the fame of the men of Iga.

These professional soldiers were actively hired by daimyos between 1485 and 1581, until Oda Nobunaga invaded Iga province and wiped out the organized clans. Survivors were forced to flee, some to the mountains of Kii, but others arrived before Tokugawa Ieyasu, where they were well treated. Some former Iga members, including Hattori Hanzo, would later serve as Tokugawa's bodyguards.

Following the Battle of Okehazama in 1560, Tokugawa employed eighty Koga ninja, led by Tomo Sukesada. They were tasked to raid an outpost of the Imagawa's. The account of this assault is given in the Mikawa Go Fudoki, where it was written that Koga ninja infiltrated the castle, set fire to its towers, and killed the castellan (governor of a castle) along with 200 of the garrison.

The Koga ninja are said to have played a role in the later Battle of Sekigahara (1600), where several hundred Koga assisted soldiers under Torii Mototada in the defense of Fushimi Castle.

After Tokugawa's victory at Sekigahara, the Iga acted as guards for the inner compounds of Edo Castle, while the Koga acted as a police force and assisted in guarding the outer gate. In 1614, the initial "winter campaign" at the Siege of Osaka saw the them in use once again.

Miura Yoemon, a ninja in Tokugawa's service, recruited shinobi from the Iga region, and sent ten of them into Osaka Castle in an effort to foster antagonism between enemy commanders. During the later "summer campaign", these hired men fought alongside regular troops at the Battle of Tennoji.

Shimabara Insurrection

A final but detailed record of their employment in open warfare occurred during the Shimabara Rebellion (1637–1638). The Koga ninja were recruited by shogun Tokugawa Iemitsu against Christian rebels led by Amakusa Shiro, who made a final stand at Hara Castle, in Hizen Province. A diary kept by a member of the Matsudairas, the Amakusa Gunki, relates: "Men from Koga in Omi Province who concealed their appearance would steal up to the castle every night and go inside as they pleased."

The Ukai diary, written by a descendant of Ukai Kanemon, has several entries describing the undercover actions taken by the Koga. They [the Koga] were ordered to scout the plan of construction of Hara Castle, and surveyed the distance from the defensive moat to the ni-no-maru (second bailey), the depth of the moat, the conditions of roads, the height of the wall, and the shape of the loopholes.

The Devastation of Hara Castle

Suspecting that the castle's supplies might be running low, the siege commander Matsudaira Nobutsuna ordered a raid on the its provisions. Here, the Koga captured bags of enemy supplies, and infiltrated the castle by night, obtaining secret passwords.

Days later, Nobutsuna ordered an information gathering mission to determine the castle's supplies. Several Koga ninjas volunteered despite being warned that chances of survival were slim. A volley of shots were fired into the sky, causing the defenders to extinguish the castle lights in preparation. Under the cloak of darkness, the shinobi concealed themselves as defenders penetrated the castle, capturing a banner of the Christian cross.

The Ukai diary writes, "we dispersed spies who were prepared to die inside Hara castle. ...those who went on the reconnaissance in force captured an enemy flag; both Arakawa Shichirobei and Mochizuki Yo'emon met extreme resistance and suffered from their serious wounds for forty days.

As the siege went on, the extreme shortage of food later reduced the defenders to eating moss and grass. This desperation would mount to futile charges by the rebels, where they were eventually defeated by the shogunate army. The Koga would later take part in conquering the castle: More and more general raids were begun, the Koga ninja band under the direct control of Matsudaira

Nobutsuna captured the ni-no-maru and the san-no-maru (outer bailey). With the fall of Hara Castle, the Shimabara Rebellion came to an end, and Christianity in Japan was forced underground." These written accounts are the last mention of ninja in war.

Undercover Agents

In the early 18th century, shogun Tokugawa Yoshimune founded the oniwaban, an agency and secret service. Members of this office, the oniwaban ("garden keeper"), were men involved in amassing details on daimyos and government officials. The secretive nature of the oniwaban—along with the earlier tradition of using Iga and Koga members as palace guards—have led some sources to define the oniwabanshu as "ninja". This portrayal is also common in later novels and jidaigeki. However, there is no written link between the earlier shinobi and the later oniwabanshu.

Duties

A page from the Shoninki (1681), detailing a list of possible disguises. In his Buke Myomokusho, military chronicler Hanawa Hokinoichi writes of the them: They traveled incognito to other territories to judge the situation of the enemy, they would cajole their way into the midst of the enemy to discover gaps, and enter enemy castles to set them on fire, and carried out assassinations, arriving in secret.

They were stealth soldiers and mercenaries hired mostly by daimyos. Their primary roles were those of espionage and sabotage, although murder was also attributed to them. In battle, the ninja could also be used to cause confusion amongst the enemy. A degree of psychological warfare in the capturing of enemy banners can be seen illustrated in the Ou Eikei Gunki, composed between the 16th and 17th centuries: Within Hataya castle there was a glorious shinobi whose skill was renowned, and one night he entered the enemy camp secretly. He took the flag from Naoe Kanetsugu's guard then returned and stood it on a high place on the front gate of the castle.

Counterintelligence

It was the chief role of the ninja. With the aid of altering, one's appearance, the they gathered information on enemy terrain and building specifications, as well as obtaining passwords and communiques.

Later in history, the Koga ninja would become regarded as agents of the Tokugawa bakufu, at a time when the bakufu used the them in a surveillance network to monitor regional daimyos as well as the Imperial court.

Vandalizing

The 16th century diary of abbot Eishun (Tamon-in Nikki) at Tamon-in monastery in Kofuku-ji describes an arson attack on a castle by men of the Iga house.

The morning, the sixth day of the 11th month of Tenbun 10, the Iga-shu entered Kasagi castle in secret and set fire to a few of the priests' quarters. They also set fire to outbuildings in various places inside the San-no-maru. They captured the Ichi-no-maru (inner bailey) and the

Ni-no-maru (castle) Entry: 26th day of the 11th month of the 10th Year of Tenbun (1541).

In 1558, Rokkaku Yoshikata employed a team of to set fire to Sawayama Castle. A chunin captain led a force of 48 shinobi into the castle by means of deception. In movements dubbed bakemono-jutsu ("ghost technique"), his men stole a lantern bearing the enemy's family crest (mon), and proceeded to make replicas with the same mon. By wielding these lanterns, they were allowed to enter the castle without a fight. Once inside, the they set fire to the castle, and Yoshitaka's army would later emerge victorious.

The diabolical nature of the shinobi is demonstrated in another arson attack soon after the burning of Sawayama Castle. In 1561, commanders acting under Kizawa Nagamasa hired three Iga ninja of genin rank to assist the conquest of a fortress in Maibara. Rokakku Yoshitaka, the same man who had hired Iga ninja just years earlier, was the fortress holder and target of attack.

The Asai Sandaiki writes of their plans: "We employed shinobi-no-mono of Iga. They were contracted to set fire to the castle". However, the mercenary shinobi were unwilling to take commands. When the fire attack did not begin as scheduled, the Iga men told the commanders, who were not from the region, that they could not possibly understand the tactics of the shinobi. They then threatened to abandon the operation if they were not allowed to act on their own strategy. The fire was eventually set, allowing Nagamasa's army to capture the fortress in a chaotic rush.

Elimination

The best-known cases of assassination attempts involve famous actual figures. Deaths of noted persons have sometimes been attributed to assassination by them, but the secretive natures of these scenarios have been difficult to prove. Assassins were often identified as ninja later on, but there is no evidence to prove whether some were specially trained for the task or simply a hired thug.

The warlord Oda Nobunaga's notorious reputation led to several attempts on his life. In 1571, a Koga ninja and sharpshooter by the name of Sugitani Zenjubo was hired to exterminate Nobunaga. Using two arquebuses, he fired two consecutive shots at Nobunaga, but was unable to inflict mortal injury through Nobunaga's protective covering. Sugitani managed to escape, but was caught four years later and put to death by torture.

In 1573, Manabe Rokuro, a vassal of daimyo Hatano Hideharu, attempted to infiltrate Azuchi Castle and kill the sleeping, Nobunaga. However, this also ended in failure, and Manabe was forced to commit suicide, after which his body was openly displayed in public. According to a document, the Iranki, when Nobunaga was inspecting Iga province, which his army had devastated, a group of three shot at him with large-caliber firearms. The shots flew wide of Nobunaga, however, and instead killed seven of his surrounding companions.

The ninja Hachisuka Tenzo was sent by Nobunaga to assassinate the powerful daimyo Takeda Shingen, but ultimately failed in his attempts. Hiding in the shadow of a tree, he avoided being seen under the moonlight, and later concealed himself in a hole he had prepared beforehand, thus escaping capture.

An attempt on Toyotomi Hideyoshi's life was also thwarted. A shinobi named Kirigakure Saizo (possibly Kirigakure Shikaemon) thrust a spear through the floorboards to kill Hideyoshi, but was unsuccessful. He was "smoked out" of his hiding place by another one working for Hideyoshi, who apparently used a sort of primitive "flamethrower". Unfortunately, the veracity of this account has been clouded by later fictional publications depicting Saizo as one of the legendary Sanada Ten Braves.

Uesugi Kenshin, the famous daimyo of Echigo Province, was rumored to have been killed by a ninja. The legend credits his death to an assassin who is said to have hidden in Kenshin's lavatory, and fatally injured Kenshin by thrusting a blade or spear into his anus. While preliminary records showed that Kenshin suffered abdominal problems, modern historians have usually attributed his death to stomach cancer, esophageal cancer, or cerebrovascular disease.

Precautionary Measures

A variety of countermeasures were taken to prevent their activities. Precautions were often taken against assassinations, such as weapons concealed in the lavatory, or under a removable floorboard. Buildings were constructed with traps and trip wires attached to alarm bells.

Japanese castles were designed to be difficult to navigate, with winding routes leading to the inner compound. Blind spots and holes in walls provided constant surveillance of these intricate paths, as exemplified in Himeji Castle.

Nijo Castle in Kyoto is constructed with long "nightingale" floors, which rested on metal hinges (uguisu-bari) specifically designed to squeak loudly when walked over. Grounds covered with gravel also provided early notice of unwanted intruders, and segregated buildings allowed fires to be better contained.

Instruction

The skills required of the shinobi have come to be known in modern times as ninjutsu, but it is unlikely they were previously named under a single discipline, yet were rather distributed among a variety of covered covert actions and survival skills. The first specialized training began in the mid-15th century, when certain samurai families started to focus on covert warfare, including reconnaissance and murder. Like the samurai, they were born into the profession, where traditions were kept in, and passed down through relatives.

Physical training was important. A certain degree of knowledge regarding common professions was also required if one was expected to take their form in disguise. Some evidence of medical training can be derived from one account, where an Iga ninja provided first-aid to Ii Naomasa, who was injured by gunfire in the Battle of Sekigahara. Here they reportedly gave Naomasa a "black medicine" meant to stop bleeding.

With the fall of the Iga and Koga clans, daimyos could no longer recruit professional ninja, and were forced to train their own shinobi. The shinobi was considered a real profession, as demonstrated in the bakufu's 1649 law on military service, which declared that only daimyos with an income of over 10,000 koku were allowed to retain shinobi. In the two centuries that followed, a number of ninjutsu manuals were written by descendants of Hattori Hanzo as well as members of the Fujibayashis, an offshoot of the Hattori. Major examples include the Ninpiden (1655), the Bansenshukai (1675), and the Shoninki (1681).

Modern schools that claim to train ninjutsu arose from the 1970s, including that of Masaaki Hatsumi (Bujinkan), Stephen K. Hayes (To-Shin Do), and Jinichi Kawakami (Banke Shinobinoden). The lineage and authenticity of these schools are a matter of controversy.

Strategy

These combatants did not always work alone. Teamwork modus operandi, exist: for example, in order to scale a wall, ninja may carry each other on their backs, or provide a human platform to assist an individual in reaching greater heights. The Mikawa Go Fudoki gives an account where a coordinated team of attackers used passwords to communicate. The account also gives a case of deception, where the attackers dressed in the same clothes as the defenders, causing much confusion. When a retreat was needed during the Siege of Osaka, they were commanded to fire upon friendly troops from behind, causing the troops to charge backwards in order to attack a perceived enemy. This tactic was used again later on as a method of crowd dispersal.

Most ninjutsu techniques recorded in scrolls and manuals revolve around ways to avoid detection, and a system for escape. These movements were loosely grouped under corresponding natural elements. Some examples are:

Hitsuke: The practice of distracting guards by starting a fire away from the ninja's planned point of entry. Falls under "fire techniques" (katon-no-jutsu).

Tanuki-gakure: The practice of climbing a tree and camouflaging oneself within the foliage. Falls under "wood techniques" (mokuton-no-jutsu).

Ukigusa-gakure: The practice of throwing duckweed over water in order to conceal underwater motion. Falls under "water techniques" (suiton-no-jutsu).

Uzura-gakure: The practice of curling into a ball and remaining motionless in order to appear like a stone. Falls under "earth techniques" (doton-no-jutsu).

Tactical martial arts ninja in sabotage and assassination was adapted for surprise attacks (night, ambush, and from behind) and for small space (thicket bush in the forest, low corridors, and small room Japanese locks, which requires short and small weapons and short strikes). In espionage one tried to avoid open battlefield with a numerically superior enemy forces, therefore their procedures were adapted to stun the enemy and escape in case of failure. A komuso monk is one of many possible costumes.

Incognito

The use of disguises is common and well documented. They could come in the form of priests, entertainers, fortune tellers, merchants, ronin, and monks. They were particularly expert at traveling in inconspicuously.

A mountain austere (yamabushi) attire facilitated travel, as they were common and could travel freely between political boundaries. The loose robes of Buddhist priests also allowed concealed weapons, such as the tanto. Minstrel or sarugaku outfits could have allowed them to spy in enemy buildings without rousing suspicion. Dressing up as a komuso, a mendicant monk known for playing the shakuhachi, was also effective, as the large "basket" hats traditionally worn by them concealed the head completely. They also ate a vegetarian diet, to avoid body odor.

Implements

Ninja utilized a large variety of tools and weaponry, some of which were commonly known, but others were more specialized. Most were tools used in the penetration of castles. A wide range of specialized equipment is described and illustrated in the 17th century Bansenshukai, including climbing equipment, extending spears, rocket-propelled arrows, and small collapsible boats.

Outer Garments

Antique Japanese gappa (travel cape) and cloth zukin (hood) with kusari (weapon) concealed underneath. While the image of a ninja clad in black garb (shinobi shozoku) is prevalent in popular media, there is no written evidence for such a costume. Instead, it was much more common for the them to impersonate civilians. The popular notion of black clothing is likely rooted in artistic convention; early drawings of ninja showed them dressed in black in order to portray a sense of invisibility.

Despite the lack of hard evidence, it has been put forward by some authorities that black robes, perhaps slightly tainted with red to hide bloodstains, was indeed the sensible garment of choice for infiltration.

Clothing used was similar to that of the samurai, but loose garments (such as leggings) were tucked into trousers or secured with belts. The tenugui, a piece of cloth also used in martial arts, had many functions. It could be used to cover the face, form a belt, or assist in climbing.

The historicity of armor specifically made for ninja cannot be ascertained. While pieces of light sheathing purportedly worn by them exist and date to the right time, there is no hard evidence of their use in various operations. Depictions of famous persons later deemed ninja often show them in samurai covering There were lightweight concealable types of shields it was made with kusari (chainmail) and small plates such as karuta that could have been worn by them including katabira (jackets) made with shells hidden between layers of cloth. Shin and arm guards, along with metal-reinforced hoods are also speculated to make up the ninja's armor.

Hardware

Tools used for infiltration are some of the most abundant artifacts related to the shinobi. A foldable ladder is illustrated in the Bansenshukai, featuring spikes at both ends to anchor it. Spiked or hooked climbing gear worn on the hands and feet also doubled as weapons. Other implements include chisels, hammers, and so forth.

The kunai was a heavy pointed tool, possibly derived from the Japanese masonry trowel, which it closely resembles. Although it is often portrayed in popular culture as a weapon, it is primarily used for digging out holes in walls. Knives and small saws (hamagari) were also used to create holes in buildings, where they served as a foothold or a passage of entry. A portable listening device (saoto hikigane) was used to eavesdrop on conversations and detect sounds.

The mizugumo was a set of wooden shoes supposedly allowing the ninja to walk on water. They were meant to work by distributing the wearer's weight over the shoes' wide bottom surface. The word mizugumo is derived from the native name for the Japanese water spider (Argyroneta aquatica japonica). The mizugumo was featured on the show MythBusters, where it was demonstrated unfit for walking on water. The ukidari, a similar footwear for walking on water, also existed in the form of a round bucket, but was probably quite unstable. Inflatable skins and breathing tubes allowed them to stay underwater for longer periods of time.

Despite the large array of tools available to the ninja, the Bansenshukai warns one not to be overburdened with equipment, stating "a successful ninja is one who uses but one tool for multiple tasks".

Armaments

Although shorter swords and daggers were used, the katana was probably their weapon of choice, and was sometimes carried on the back. The katana had several uses beyond normal combat. In dark places, the scabbard could be extended out of the sword, and used as a long probing device.

The sword could also be laid against the wall, where one could use the sword guard (tsuba) to gain a higher foothold. The katana could even be used as a device to stun enemies before attacking them, by putting a combination of red pepper, dirt or dust, and iron filings into the area near the top of the scabbard, so that as the sword was drawn the concoction would fly into the enemy's eyes, stunning him until a lethal blow could be made. While straight swords were used before the invention of the katana, the straight ninjato has no historical precedent and is likely a modern invention.

An array of darts, spikes, knives, and sharp, star-shaped discs were known collectively as shuriken. They were not exclusive to the shinobi, but used more so by the Samurai, where they could be thrown in any direction.

Bows were used for sharpshooting; some were intentionally made smaller than the traditional yumi (longbow). The chain and sickle (kusarigama) were also utilized. This weapon consisted of a weight on one end of a chain, and a sickle (kama) on the other. The weight was swung to injure or disable an opponent, and the sickle used to kill at close range. Simple gardening tools such as the kunai and sickles were used as weaponry so that, if discovered, one could claim they are his tools and not weapons, despite their effectiveness to be used in battle.

Incendiary devices were introduced around the 13th century. These gadgets were designed to release smoke or poison gas, along with fragmentation explosives packed with iron or pottery shrapnel.

Along with common weapons, a large assortment of miscellaneous arms were associated with the ninja. Some examples include poison, makibishi (caltrops), cane swords (shikomizue), land mines, fukiya (blowguns), poisoned darts, acid-spurting tubes, and firearms. The happo, a small eggshell filled with blinding powder (metsubushi), was also used to facilitate escape.

Deceptive Skills

Superhuman or supernatural powers were often associated with the ninja with a style of Japanese martial arts in ninjutsu. Some legends include flight, invisibility, shape shifting, teleportation, the potential to "split" into multiple bodies (bunshin), the summoning of animals (kuchiyose), and control over the five classical elements. These fabulous notions have stemmed from popular imagination regarding the ninja's mysterious status, as well as romantic ideas found in later Japanese art of the Edo period. Magical artistry was rooted in their own misinformation efforts to disseminate fanciful information. For example, Nakagawa Shoshunjin, the 17th-century founder of Nakagawa-ryū, claimed in his own writings (Okufuji Monogatari) that he had the ability to transform into birds and animals.

Kuji-Kiri

Kuji-kiri ("nine symbolic cuts") is a practice of using hand gestures found today in Shugendō and Shingon Mikkyō. It is also present in some old and traditional schools ("ryūha") of Japanese martial arts including but not exclusive to schools that have ties with ninjutsu.

This is an esoteric method which, when performed with an array of hand "seals" (kuji-in), was meant to allow the ninja to enact stupendous feats.

The kuji ("nine characters") is a concept originating from Taoism, where it was a string of nine words used in charms and incantations. In China, this tradition mixed with Buddhist beliefs, assigning each of the nine words to a Buddhist deity.

The kuji may have arrived in Japan via Buddhism, where it flourished within Shugendō. Here too, each word in the kuji was associated with Buddhist deities, animals from Taoist mythology, and later, Shinto kami. The mudrā, a series of hand symbols representing different Buddhas, was applied to the kuji by Buddhists, possibly through the esoteric Mikkyō teachings. The yamabushi ascetics of Shugendō adopted this practice, using the hand gestures in spiritual, healing, and exorcism rituals.

Later, the use of kuji passed onto certain bujutsu (martial arts) and ninjutsu schools, where it was said to have many purposes. The application of kuji to produce a desired effect was called "cutting" (kiri) the kuji. Intended effects range from physical and mental concentration, to more incredible claims about rendering an opponent immobile, or even the casting of magical spells. These legends were captured in popular culture, which interpreted the kuji-kiri as a precursor to magical acts.

International Ninja

On February 25, 2018, Yamada Yūji, the professor of Mie University and chronicler Nakanishi Gō announced that they had identified three people who were successful in early modern Ureshino, including the ninja Benkei Musō. Musō is thought to be the same person as Denrinbō Raikei, the Chinese disciple of Marume Nagayoshi. It came as a shock when the existence of a foreign samurai was verified by authorities.

Celebrated People

Many famed individuals in Japanese history have been associated or identified as ninja, but their status is difficult to prove and may be the product of later imagination. Rumors surrounding famous warriors, such as Kusunoki Masashige or Minamoto no Yoshitsune sometimes describe them as ninja, but there is little evidence for these claims.

DID YOU KNOW?

Here Are Some Other Interesting Fun Facts about Ninjas

WHY WERE THEY REPORTED TO HAVE THE ABILITY TO WALK ON WATER? What observers were unaware of is that stones were strategically placed underwater by them which were not visible to the naked eye by observers.

WERE THEY EXPERT MIND READERS? Some reports suggest that they were expert mind readers. But this was never proven to have any truth behind it.

HOW DID THEY UNDERTAKE A WALL? Some reports suggest that they used a spring board device to propel them over a wall. But it is doubtful that such scientific ingenuity existed back in those days. What is more likely that they would use a long pole to surmount a wall, like a track & field pole vaulter.

SHOULDER DISLOCATION. In their youth when bones were soft the ninja learned to stretch and manipulate joints so that he might dislocate them. This strange skill came into use in the event he was captured or needed to squeeze through small openings.

STEALTH WALKING. The primary walking move, the shinobi-ashi was to walk carefully and with poise, first placing the fourth, then middle toe on the ground and smoothly rolling down to the heel. The shinobi-ashi was a great walk when time was in abundance, as the gentle and flowing nature of the foot roll allowed almost silent movement.

HOW DID THEY CONFUSE OPPONENTS? They were said to use a sidestepping movement to confuse opponents. By keeping the feet placed in a forward position they would cross over with either left foot or the right foot then repeat that movement several times as needed.

HIDING IN TOILETS. Ninjas were said to hide in toilets to murder someone while in wait of their intended victim. Whether or not that ever occurred in anyone's guess.

TRAPPING A SURE-FOOTED NINJA. The method of rolling a round sphere across the ground (perhaps a rock or wooden ball) was used to trap a sure-footed ninja who would leap out of the path. An ordinary citizen might not be skilled in this, and the object might simply bounce off their foot.

THEY MIGHT WORK IN PAIRS. One would cause a distraction which enabled his partner to perform their task or enter a castle.

CONDITIONING HANDS FOR COMBAT. They were said to practice striking with the edge of hands and palms on trees to condition them for fighting.

POISONING WATER. Ninjas were said to use wolfsbane to poison water wells of their enemies. It is one of the most toxic plants, the toxins in Wolfsbane can cause a slowing of heart rate which could be fatal, and even eating a very small amount can lead to an upset stomach. Its poison can also act through contact with the skin, particularly through open wounds.

NINJUTSU AND SOLITARY PRACTICE? It offers a benefit that other martial arts do not. It can be practiced alone and does not require a partner as does judo, aikido, or jiujitsu. This is true whether you are doing strength or flexibility exercises, or practicing with a sword, broom handle, or similar object to mimic a weapon.

THEIR DUTIES. Information gathering, stealth, scouting, embedding themselves among the enemy, propaganda, spreading falsehoods, sewing chaos and sabotage, plus counterintelligence.

HOW DID RUMORS BEGIN? For example, someone might witness the escape of a ninja by pursuant enemy, flying thru trees unawares that the ninja had pre-tied a series of ropes in the trees that they could swing upon.

DID ALL OF THEM CARRY SWORDS? Some may have preferred a spear instead. It has a longer reach than a sword, which therefor offers certain advantages in combat.

DID THEY WEAR TABI BOOTS? When you see those black split-toe shoes, called Tabi, they are normally in films where ninja are climbing walls and spying on important people to gain information. Back in the 15th century, Japan began importing cotton from their nearby neighbor, China.

The new fabric gave birth to innovative products, like socks. The Geta, a shoe that looks like a flat wooden platform sandal with a leather thong strap, was the footwear of choice, and new socks had to fit their structure. The result was creating an ankle-height cotton sock with a separation between the big toe and the rest of the foot. Essentially, the original Tabi.

WHAT DID THEY DO WHEN BEING CHASED BY PURSUERS? They employed the use of caltrops. Small triangular shaped metal objects of iron tossed out by ninja in the path of pursuers. Stepping on these would penetrate the soles of the foot and cripple them in great pain.

DID THEY SOMETIMES USE SCARY MASKS TO FRIGHTEN THE ENEMY? YES!

COULD THEY COULD DISAPPEAR IN A PUFF OF SMOKE? No! That was the Hollywood version.

WERE THEY THE ENEMY OF THE SAMURAI? No! Ninja was hired by various Samurai classes to fight against other Samurai.

DID THEY ORIGINATE IN JAPAN? This may be false. Ancient records suggest that ninja-like operatives were present several thousand years ago in China. They may have performed similar functions as the ninja such as espionage, etc.

COULD THEY PUT THEIR EAR TO THE GROUND TO DETERMINE IF BEING FOLLOWED BY RIDERS ON HORSEBACK? Most likely it was false. No one really knows if this is truly possible or not.

FINALE

All civilizations, and especially armies, have sent out spies to view potential enemies since time began. Why the ninja rose to predominance is quite a curious thing. Was it the black or unique uniform and sword that brought them to the forefront?

Therefore, should we find it strange that, say a teenager or an adult, would want to dress up in a ninja costume and desire to brandish a wooden, plastic, or even a real sword?

Would the same be asked about someone who joins the military and is proud of wearing a military uniform? Or the one who undertakes intensive training or fighting in combat in order to earn a badge of honor?

How about those who attend a masquerade ball and selects a costume that fits their personality?

What is so captivating about becoming a ninja today? Well, humans don't have super powers like Superman or Spider man, but they can imagine themselves as a ninja if they had a black or the costume, a sword, and some throwing stars. If you watch various social media platforms you will find an abundance of kids and young adults pretending to be a ninja with their friends or acquaintances. This includes American Civil war imitators and the early mountain men who explored the American west. Just consider all this as food for thought.

END

GLOSSARY

Aikido/Aiki-jujutsu: originally called Daitō-ryū Aikido: a form of self-defense and martial art that uses locks, holds, throws opponent's own movements.

Baku: an abbreviation of bakufu, meaning "military government"

Bamboo Cane/shaft: hollow bamboo shafts were used for concealing blades, chains, various powders, maps and secret

Bansenshukai: a book containing a collection of knowledge and information

Bo: a long staff.

Bokken: is used as an inexpensive wooden and relatively safe substitute for a real sword in several martial arts

Budo: term describing modern Japanese martial arts."Martial Way", "Way of War" or the "Way of Martial Arts".

Bujutsu: martial art, military science, or military strategy.

Bushido: Samurai code of conduct.

Caste: hereditary, social class.

Castellan: governor of a castle.

Daimyo: feudal lord.

Dojo: a school for training in various forms of self-defense.

Doshin: half Samurai.

Five basic elements: earth, water, fire, air, and space.

Fukiya: blow gun.

Fuma Clan: horse mounted guerrilla fighters.

Garrote: a rope, scarf or chain used for strangling.

Genjutsu: techniques of illusion or sleight of hand.

Hanbo: a short staff.

Hara Kiri or seppuku: mean exactly the same thing in Japanese, but, Japanese people almost never use the word harakiri and prefer the word seppuku instead. Harakiri refers to the action of cutting stomach while seppuku represents the ritual and the traditional procedure of cutting the stomach. Seppuku was a highly ritualized exercise limited to the Japanese warrior caste, the samurai, with its sanctioned practice spanning from the 700s until it was formally outlawed in 1873.

Iga: Iga and Koga clans produced professional ninja, specifically trained for their mercenary roles.

Jo: a medium staff.

Jutte or Jitte: a martial arts weapon similar to the Sai. However, while the Sai is traditionally used in pairs, the Jutte is a single weapon.

Kagimono-kiki: the word "Shinobi" is a much better term to find historical reference to the ninja as we know it. The Hojo Godai-ki uses other terms for ninja such as rappa and seppa, while the Koyo Gunkan uses kagimono-kiki.

Kagina: grappling hook

Kama: a traditional Japanese farming implement like a sickle or billhook used for reaping crops and employed as a weapon.

Kanch: a spy

Kanji: are Chinese character, one of the three scripts used in the Japanese language.

Katana: sword characterized by a curved, single-edged blade with a circular or squared guard and long grip to accommodate two hands.

Kenpo: Chinese martial art using bare hands and weapons.

Kishu: surprise attacker

Koga: the Iga and Koga clans produced professional ninja, specifically trained for their mercenary roles.

Konran: an agitator

Kunai: primarily digging tools, and when used as weapons, were stabbing, and thrusting implements.

Kunoichi: female ninja.

Kuroko: stage hands in traditional Japanese theater.

Kusari fundo: a chain weapon.

Kusarigama: a type of metal chain (kusari) or sickle with a heavy iron weight attached.

Kyoketsu-Shoge: a double-edged blade attached to 12-18 feet of rope, chain, or hair which then ends in a small metal ball.

Metsubushi: blinding powder.

Mizugumo: a water crossing device used by ninja.

Ninjitsu: It is actually pronounced ninjutsu, but it's hard to tell the difference so people often say ninjitsu. But that is not technically correct. Both refer to the spy craft used by the elite samurai. The ninja, or shinobi, were the samurai equivalent to the Special Forces.

Ninjutsu or Ninpo: In English, ninjutsu means "the art of remaining unseen" or "the invisible art".

Rappa: The Hojo Godai-ki uses other terms for ninja such as rappa and seppa, while the Koyo Gunkan uses.

Ronin: drifter or wanderer, a type of samurai who had no lord or master. A samurai becomes a rōnin upon the death of his master, or after the loss of his master's favor or legal privilege.

Seppa: The use of spacers in the Japanese katana sword. These Brass katana Seppa are the washers or spacers that go either side of the Tsuba on a katana. Below the habaki on the blade side and above the Fuchi on the handle side. Their role is to help tighten up the fittings of the sword, therefore they are not just for decoration but have an important function.

Shinai: a sword typically made of bamboo used for practice and competition in kendo.

Shinobi: aka ninja, meaning "those who act in stealth". Walk carefully and patiently.

Shogunate: the hereditary military dictatorship of Japan (1192–1867).

Shoninki: ninja manual (True Path of the Ninja) written in 1681.

Shuko: climbing claws or claw weapon.

Shuriken: "hidden hand blade" is a concealed weapon that was used as a hidden dagger.

Skullduggery: underhanded or unscrupulous behavior; trickery.

Soke: a term that means "the head family (house)

Taijutsu: (literally "body technique" or "body skill") is a Japanese martial art blanket term for any combat skill, technique or system of martial art using body movements that are described as an empty-hand combat skill or system.

Tantō: a short sword worn by the samurai of feudal Japan. These were designed to primarily be stabbing weapons, but the razor edge could also slash cut as well.

Teisatsu: a scout

Tessen: is a Japanese hand fan designed for use in warfare.

Tetsubishi/Caltrops: a weapon made up of two or more sharp nails or spines arranged in a manner that one of them always points upward from a stable base.

Wakizashi: reference to the practice of wearing this item inserted through one's obi or sash at one's side.

Ya: is the Japanese word for arrow.

Yamabushi: hermits of the mountains

Yari: the term for a traditionally-made Japanese blade in the form of a spear, or more specifically, the straight-headed spear.

Yumi: a bow (archery).

Zukin: scarf or hood.

REFERENCES

Ninja: The True Story of Japan's Secret Warrior Cult Turnbull, Stephen R. 1991

"Ninja: AD 1460-1650." Oxford: Turnbull, Stephen (2003). Osprey Publishing.

"The Ninja: An Invented Tradition?" Stephen Turnbull. Published in The Journal of Global Initiatives: Policy, Pedagogy, Interdisciplinary Reflections on Japan, 2014.

The Lost Samurai School: Secrets of Mubyoshi Ryu Paperback - October 25, 2016 Antony Cummins.

In Search of the Ninja: The Historical Truth of Ninjutsu. Stroud, Gloucestershire, The History Press, 2012.

Samurai and Ninja: The Real Story Behind the Japanese Warrior Myth.

The Book of Ninja: The first complete translation of the Bansenshukai, 2013, Antony Cummins & Yoshie Minami

Iga and Koka Ninja Skills: The Secret Shinobi Scrolls of Chikamatsu Shigenori. Paperback-October 1, 2014 Antony Cummins

The Secret Traditions of the Shinobi: Hattori Hanzo's Shinobi Hiden and Other Ninja Scrolls Paperback - November 27, 2012 Antony Cummins

True Path of the Ninja: The Definitive Translation of the Shoninki (The Authentic Ninja Training Manual) Paperback – March 14, 2017 Antony Cummins. Tuttle Publishing.

Ninjutsu: History and Tradition Paperback - Unabridged, June, 1981 Masaaki Hatsumi.

Ninja Secrets from the Grandmaster Paperback – November, 1987 Masaaki Hatsumi.

Essence of Ninjutsu Paperback – April 1, 1988 Masaaki Hatsumi.

The Ninja and Their Secret Fighting Art Paperback August 1, 2017 Stephen K. Hayes

Ninja Vol.2: The Warriors Way of Enlightenment Stephen K. Hayes

The Mystic Arts of the Ninja Paperback – April 1, 1985 Stephen Hayes

Ninja Volume 1: Spirit of the Shadow Warrior Paperback -November 1, 1980 Stephen Hayes

Ninjutsu: The Art of Invisibility (Facts, Legends, and Techniques) (Tuttle Martial Arts) Paperback – May 15, 2008 Donn F. Draeger

Comrehensive Asian Fighting Arts (Bushido—The Way of the Warrior) Paperback – January 15, 1981 Donn F. Draeger

Classical Bujutsu (Martial Arts and Ways of Japan) Paperback December 18, 2007 Donn F. Draeger

Tiger Scroll of the Koga Ninja. Sensei, Jay. 1985

Spike and Chain: Japanese Fighting Arts Hardcover 1968 Charles V. Gruzanski

Ninja Attack! True Tales of Assassins, Samurai, and Outlaws Paperback – July 10, 2012 Hiroko Yoda, Matt Alt, Tuttle Publishing

"Ninja: The Invisible Assassins". Adams, Andrew (1970). Ohara Press.

Martial Arts of the World: an encyclopedia, 2001, Thomas A. Green.

The Ninja Museum of Igaryu located in Iga, Mie Prefecture, Japan

Illuminati Disclosure (20 April 2015). Ancient Warfare: Shinobi Ninjas and Kung Fu Shaolin Monks

A Complete Guide to Koryu Jujutsu. Classical Fighting Arts of Japan: Mol, Serge (June 6, 2001).

Taijutsu: Ninja Art of Unarmed Combat Paperback – November, 1986 Charles Daniel.

Art of the Ninja – August, 1988 Peter Lewis

Secrets of the samurai: a survey of the martial arts of feudal Japan, Ratti, Oscar Westbrook, Adele (1991), Tuttle Publishing

Takamatsu: The Man Who Taught Ninjutsu to Today's Ninja Leader. Black Belt Magazine. June 1985.

The Last Shinobi. Ettig, Wolfgang (2006).

Takamatsu Toshitsugu Tengu-Publishing.

Black Belt Magazine June 1987

Black Belt Magazine August 1967

The Art of War Paperback – October 26, 1988 Sun Tzu

The Book of Five Rings, Sep 1, 2010 Miyamoto Musashi, Ninja Documentary, History Channel

Secret History of the Ninja Uncovered. National Geographic Documentary.

Samurai TV Series, Shintaro.

Ninja Unmasking the Myth. Stephen Turnbull.

Ninja Skills, Antony Cummins.

Ninja Truths & Myths.

The Illustrated Ninja Handbook. Remigiusz Borda.

'The Octagon' 1980, American Cinema Productions

Sho Kosugi in 'Revenge of the Ninja', 1983

Cannon Films

* Famed Ninjas Who Actually Existed. Wikipedia.

** NINJA: An Encapsulation of Ninja Lore and History. This article has been shortened for brevity's sake. If you wish to read it in its entirety visit Wikipedia.com

Author Profile

An author of numerous magazine articles on various topics prior to turning to novels, Lex Lyon is a graduate of the Institute of Applied Science for scientific crime detection. He received his on-the-job police training from the Fayetteville Police Department in North Carolina. A former Army paratrooper trained as an infantryman and sniper; he was also a Golden Glove boxer, martial arts practitioner, and student of ancient and modern weaponry. A member of the Christian faith, his hobbies and interests include reading, sports, and fitness.

Other Books by Author Lex Lyon

'BE PREPARED!' tells the reader how to avoid being the target of criminals along with valuable tips on home security, safe travel, street smarts, car-jacking, terrorist attacks, identity theft, wilderness survival, self-defense tricks, weaponry, remaining safe in a natural disaster like flood, fire, or tornado ... even a chapter on preventive health care, how to keep your pets safe ... and so much more!